STAMP-A-CHRISTMAS ™

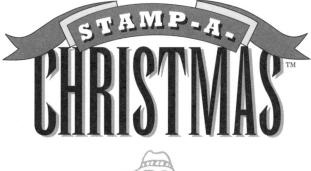

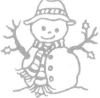

STAMP-A-

CHRISTMAS ™

Judy Ritchie, Kate Schmidt,
and Jamie Kilmartin
Stamp designs by Judy Pelikan

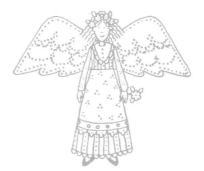

HUGH LAUTER LEVIN ASSOCIATES, INC.

Stamp designs © 1995 by Judy Pelikan
Line drawings by Susan Swan

Design by Kathleen Herlihy-Paoli,
Inkstone Design

All of the *Stamp-A-Christmas*™ projects have been created by Judy Ritchie,
of The Great American Stamp Store in Westport, CT

Printed in Hong Kong
ISBN 0-88363-319-1

Stamp-A-Christmas™ is a trademark of All Night Media, Inc., San Rafael, CA.
and is used under license. All Night Media, Inc., is a complete manufacturer
and supplier of rubber stamps, equipment and supplies
that are available at your local book store, stamp store,
or gift and stationery store.

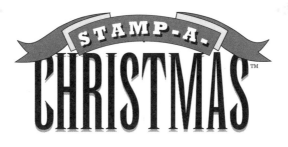
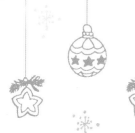
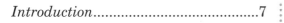

INTRODUCTION

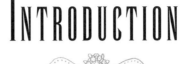

$\mathcal{C}$reating beautiful stationery, cards, gifts, and packaging is well within the range of everyone's abilities when you create with rubber stamps. You do not have to be an artist to express your creative talents. Rubber stamping is fun, easy, and rewarding, and offers a wide range of outlets for creative expression. It is also a perfect activity to fit into today's busy lifestyles. For young and old alike, stamping can be enjoyed alone or in groups. All you need is a few stamps, an ink pad, papers, markers, a few accessories and you're ready to start.

$\mathcal{T}$he *Stamp-A-Christmas*™ kit contains 21 art rubber stamps with a Christmas theme; a green ink pad; red, green, and black brush markers; red, yellow, and green colored pencils; and gold glitter glue to enhance your designs. Also included in the kit is a sampling of papers including cards, envelopes, and gift tags/tree ornaments and gold thread. With this kit you will be able to produce marvelous creative projects with Christmas and winter themes. Just take a few minutes now to learn the basics of stamping. Once you have read the first few sections of this guide you will know everything you need to create artwork that will impress your family and friends as well as professional stampers. We all love to receive handmade cards and gifts, and working with rubber stamps gives you the opportunity to create professional-looking works of art created just for the recipient.

All the stamps in the *Stamp-A-Christmas*™ kit have been specially designed to work together in this kit, as well as complement the rest of your stamp collection. We wanted you to have a set of stamps with a distinctive style but also one in which the stamps could be used in several different ways.

Stamps are magically versatile tools. By combining them in different ways you can achieve many different looks, a new one every time. Look in the *Stamp-A-Christmas*™ Special Projects section of this book to see how we have combined some of the stamps.

Using the stamps in different ways and in different combinations will not only provide you with more images to work with, but it will also help you to stretch your own imagination and tap your creativity.

What is a Christmas scene without a magnificent, decorated Christmas tree? We designed our tree stamp to fit in and work with the other stamps in the kit. It can be used alone, and you can also create a fabulous tree from multiple impressions of the single tree stamp. Then have fun decorating the tree with the other stamps in the kit.

We hope this inspires you to use your stamps creatively. The pine bough, for example, can be used as a single sprig or bough, as a swag, or as a full wreath. You have everything you need in this kit to make literally hundreds of projects. We hope to encourage you to see possibilities. Don't be limited by what you have. Explore every possibility.

These are Christmas stamps, but they need not be used for Christmas projects only. The angels, for instance, can be used all year long, the stars are not seasonal, and several trees together could be a woods, and so on.

We offer you ideas and techniques for making stamped projects. Surprise and delight your family and friends with your own clever and original cards and presents handstamped by you.

Be creative and have fun.

GETTING STARTED

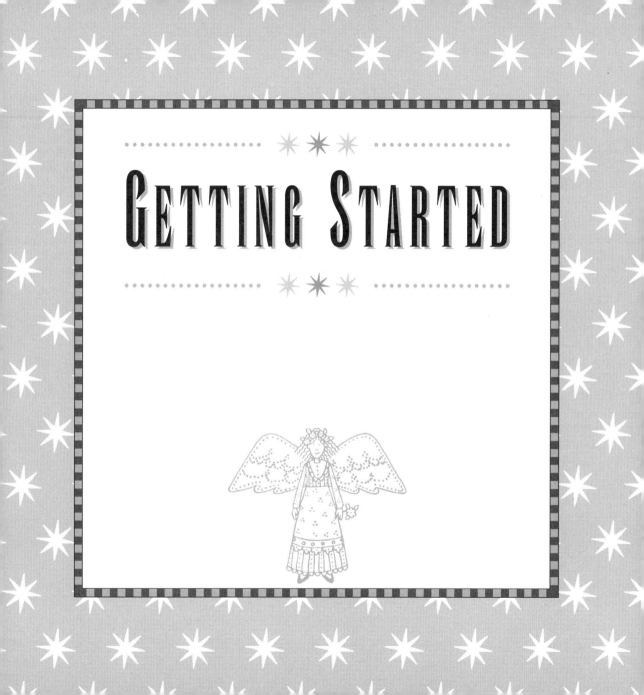

GETTING STARTED WITH THE STAMP-A-CHRISTMAS™ KIT

*W*e have provided you with materials to make dozens of interesting projects, but don't hesitate to use these stamps in combination with other inks, markers, paper, glitter, or even with other stamps that you have.

*M*any stampers prefer working with wood-mounted rubber stamps. To mount the stamps from this kit on wood see page 61 or you can have someone at your local rubber stamp store mount them on wood for you.

*T*o make your stamped images as neat as possible before stamping on your final paper, check that there is enough ink on the image, and that there is no stray ink around the edges of the rubber die. Remove any ink from around the unraised portions of the rubber stamp with a damp paper towel before stamping.

Season's Greetings

THE *STAMP-A-CHRISTMAS*™ KIT

The first step in using the *Stamp-A-Christmas*™ kit is to break apart, along the perforations, the stamps included in the kit. You will want to label or index the stamps so that you can identify them quickly as you use them.

To prepare the labels, peel away the stamp images from the sticker paper that was sitting on top of the stamps in the kit. Position and stick the cut-out label onto the top of the appropriate stamp, making sure the stamp is oriented in the same direction as the stamp image. If you wish to protect the labels, cover each with heavy transparent packing tape or clear contact paper. Trim the excess tape flush with the stamp block.

*R*emember to store your stamps rubber die-side down, out of direct sunlight, and away from heat and dust. Sunlight and excess heat can harden the rubber.

*B*efore you begin to stamp prepare a work area. You can

Stamp designs © 1995 by Judy Pelikan

achieve the best results and sharpest images by working on a cushioned surface. A pad of newsprint, a computer mouse pad, or a magazine will all work fine. The newsprint pad is especially helpful because it can function as a cushion and scrap paper at the same time.

*T*he type of image on a stamp dictates how you should stamp so that the whole design will print evenly. For example, large stamps, or stamps with large solid areas require more ink and pressure than finely detailed stamps. Apply pressure evenly as you stamp directly down on the paper. For large images, hold the

Hold the stamp firmly with one hand and press down on the stamp rotating your finger evenly across the back of the stamp.

stamp with one hand while pressing evenly on the top of the stamp with the other. Be careful not to rock or wiggle the stamp, or the image will be blurred.

*B*ecause each stamp has its own peculiarities (some stampers might even say "personality"), it is important to make test prints on scrap paper before stamping on your good paper.

*T*he ink pad included in this kit contains a water-based dye ink for use on all types of paper. The pad can be re-inked when it runs dry. Store your ink pad upside down to bring the ink to the surface. This way your pad will always be ready to use. Some stampers store their ink pads in the refrigerator to retard evaporation. The water-based brush markers in this kit contain the same ink as the ink pad and therefore are usable on all papers. Remember to cap your markers when they are not in use to prevent them from drying out.

Before you begin to stamp, you should have a cleaning plate ready to clean the ink off each stamp as you finish with it. To prepare a cleaning plate moisten a paper towel, sponge, or small rag with warm water, wring it out, and place it on a plate.

Be sure to clean the ink off of each stamp before you switch to another color, or when you are finished stamping. To clean the stamp, stamp the image several times on scrap paper to remove as much ink as possible. Then tap the stamp (image side down) onto the cleaning plate and, finally, onto a clean, dry paper towel to remove excess moisture.

Never use harsh cleaners or alcohol based solvents to clean your stamps. They could leave a film on the stamp or dry out the rubber. If the ink seems particularly stubborn, you might try scrubbing the rubber with an old toothbrush dipped in water. To remove ink from your hands, try baby wipes, or soap and water.

Two kinds of paper are included with this kit. The note cards are wood free with a matte finish and the die-cut gift tags/tree ornaments are coated with a glossy finish. You can stamp on almost any smooth-surfaced paper. Note how the ink from both the ink pad and the markers works with these papers. Experiment with other papers to find what you like best. Use the papers in this kit as a reference when purchasing additional papers for stamping.

Cleaning a stamp using a handy cleaning plate.

$\mathcal{W}$e have provided markers in the *Stamp-A-Christmas*™ kit, so you do not have to ink every bit of every stamp. There may be times when you will want to use only a part of a stamp. In fact, these 21 stamps become many more if you use them creatively. With the *Stamp-A-Christmas*™ stamps, for instance, you don't have to use all of the snowflakes; you could use one or two. You don't have to use Santa and the present every time; you can use one or the other. You could use the pine cone without the bough; you could repeat the small holly sprig on the "To/From" stamp by itself. There are many options which will be fun to exercise as you gain confidence as a stamper.

$\mathcal{D}$on't overlook the colored pencils provided in the *Stamp-A-Christmas*™ kit. The subtle shading and soft color can add another level of sophistication to your stamped art.

SUPPLIES YOU'LL NEED

✳ In addition to the items found in the *Stamp-A-Christmas*™ kit, assemble the following items before you start your projects:

✳ scissors

✳ pad of paper, or some other cushioning surface

✳ X-Acto knife, or mat knife

✳ scrap paper

✳ card stock or index cards

✳ sticky notes or thin paper for masking

✳ wet paper towels on a plate

✳ glue or double-sided cellophane tape, double-sided foam tape

✳ uncoated matte finish gift wrap, and plain tissue paper

✳ uncoated matte finish lunch bags

✳ ruler

✳ hole punch

STAMPING TECHNIQUES

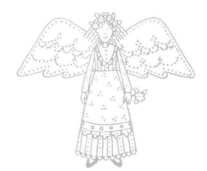

INKING WITH AN INK PAD

*T*ap the stamp gently a few times into the ink pad and then check to make sure the whole image is covered with ink. If you are too forceful when tapping the stamp on the ink pad, you may get ink on the rubber area surrounding the image. This could lead to unwanted stray marks on your paper.

*T*o achieve a lighter or more subtle shade of ink, stamp first on scrap paper before stamping the image on your "good" paper. Use this technique to make a background design to appear under other stamped images, or to make attractive stationery with a subtle overall design.

*P*ractice inking your stamps and stamping a few impressions on scrap paper and on an extra sheet of good paper a few times to learn the idiosyncracies of each stamp. Some of the images need more ink than others; some need less.

*A*lways keep your stamp pad closed when not in use to prevent the pad from drying out. Store your ink pad upside down so the ink stays at the surface.

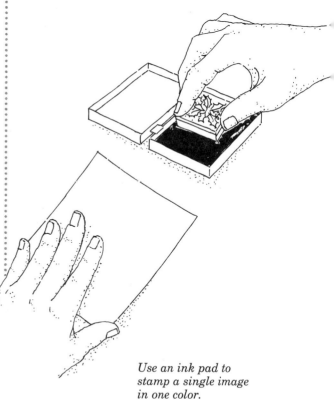

Use an ink pad to stamp a single image in one color.

INKING WITH WATER-BASED MARKERS

*A*n alternative to using an ink pad, and our favorite way to work, is with water-based brush markers. Hold the stamp in one hand with the rubber die facing up, and color or paint directly onto the raised stamped image with one or more colored markers. Work quickly to keep the ink from drying. If necessary, breathe gently on the stamp (with an open-mouthed "HAH") to add moisture to the ink just before stamping. Depending on the paper you are using, you may be able to get a second impression without re-inking the stamp. You might be able to simply breathe on the stamp once again. You will soon be able to judge when you need to re-ink a stamp. Just practice with each stamp a few times, and it will all become second nature to you in a very short time.

USING BRUSH MARKERS ALLOWS YOU TO:

✳ Stamp in a wide range of colors that are not readily available in ink pads.

✳ Stamp a multicolored image by applying different colors to various parts of the stamp.

✳ Stamp a portion of an image.

*W*hen inking the stamp, be sure to brush over the entire image you wish to print with the side of the marker. Always ink a lighter color before a darker color to avoid getting darker ink on the light marker. If you find that you have excess ink on the paper after stamping, simply turn your finished artwork over and blot it lightly on a piece of scrap paper.

*B*e *sure* that the markers you use on your stamps are water-based. Permanent ink may harm the rubber on the stamp.

Color different parts of the stamp with different color inks.

PLANNING YOUR LAYOUT

$\mathcal{S}$ome artwork looks so right you would think it just happened that way—the way the cliffs meet the sea, or a wildflower pops out of the earth at just the right spot on a summer morning. But, of course, we mortals have to plan our designs. And, frankly, this is probably the most exciting part of creating a project. Now is the time to decide what you are saying with your artwork. What do you want the recipi-ent of your card to feel, for instance? We all know that bright colors are cheerful, soft pastels soothing, and dark colors elicit a more somber or dignified response. But did you realize that where you place an image on a page has as much effect on the viewer as the colors you choose?

$\mathcal{T}$he visual placement of objects on a card or package can be unpredictable and exciting, predictable and soothing, or reliable. Just as the tilt of a head or a hand can be an inviting or a dismissing gesture, so too can the orientation of a

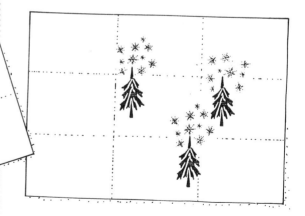

Dividing your space into thirds horizontally and vertically can produce interesting layouts.

This card, with three impressions of the holly bough, offers a strong statement.

always. Look at most of the old master paintings, for instance. The focal point is not usually dead center.

*O*ne trick that we use constantly in planning our layouts is to divide the space into thirds horizontally and vertically (make a tic-tac-toe board). And then move the stamp images around within the quadrants. The most interesting visual points are near the intersecting lines, so arrange your design around one or more of those focal points, filling in the background as needed. Please don't feel compelled to fill up all the white space on your card. Space is as important a design element as any of the stamps.

*O*n a practical note, be sure to plan your layout on scrap paper. Stamp the images on paper; then cut them out and place them on a grid. These cut-outs are easy to move around as you finalize your design.

*Y*ou should also test the colors of your inks, pencils, and markers to see how they will work together. Test colors on the same kind of paper you'll be using for your finished project.

figure in your artwork. Look at the stationery we made with the gingerbread man literally dancing across the top of the page. It makes you smile. It might even make you feel like dancing!

*T*his is all a way of saying that you can direct the effect of your work by being aware of certain basic design concepts.

*P*lacing a design element (one of our stamps) right in the middle of your card can sometimes be effective—but not

COLORING IN

*W*hen you are using stamps that are primarily an outline, you can achieve charming results by coloring in the image after it is stamped. See our Christmas tree ball ornaments or the bow, for example, both of which are outline drawings, as opposed to the holly or the large star, both of which are solid images.

*S*tamp the image with a dark ink on any kind of paper if you are going to color with markers. If you are going to use colored pencils, you *must* stamp on matte or non-glossy paper. When the ink is dry, color in the image on your paper just as you would in a coloring book. Use fine line markers to create bright colors, and colored pencils to achieve a softer look.

*W*ith colored pencils you can achieve gradations of color. The harder you press, the darker the color will appear. Colored pencils often look better against a soft outline, which you can create by using the technique outlined earlier: that is, press the stamp on the ink pad, tap it once lightly on scrap paper, and then stamp the image onto your paper. For example, if you are using black ink, this method will give you a gray outline.

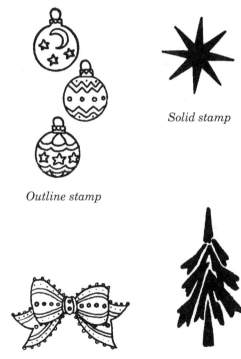

Outline stamp

Solid stamp

Outline stamp

Solid stamp

SPARKLE

$\mathcal{A}$dd excitement, sophistication, and sparkle to your projects with glitter-filled glue. Apply the glitter glue to accentuate specific areas of your stamped design. The gold glitter glue in our *Stamp-A-Christmas*™ kit is very easy to use. Simply tip the container upside down and gently squeeze the bottle as you drag the tip along the line, or dab lightly on the spot you wish to highlight. Allow the glue to dry for two to four hours.

$\mathcal{G}$litter glue is great for filling in or outlining stamped images. You can create backgrounds and borders or write in a name or whole message.

$\mathcal{I}$f our glitter glue is not glittery enough for you, sprinkle additional dry glitter on the image after applying the glitter glue.

$\mathcal{S}$tars can twinkle with the addition of gold glitter glue. The application of glitter should be the last step in the execution of your project.

$\mathcal{N}$ever put glue directly on the rubber stamp die, since it would ruin the rubber. If your stamp should pick up some glitter, you can remove it by tapping the sticky side of a piece of transparent tape on the rubber die.

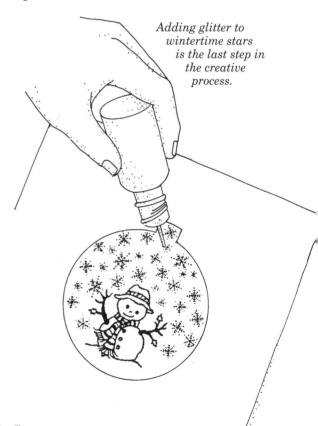

Adding glitter to wintertime stars is the last step in the creative process.

REPEATED IMAGES

A charming border of trees is complemented by glitter stars.

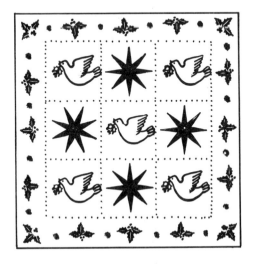

One stamp can go a long way when it is used to make patterns, borders, or clusters. Use the same color ink and stamp across the bottom, up both sides, or all around the edges of a card to create a pattern or border. Try alternating colors for variety. Or stamp one design repeated all over the card to create a background pattern or texture. If you change the angle of the stamp as you work you do not have to worry about aligning the images perfectly.

It is important to consider the size of the stamps you use together when they are used as borders or patterns. Stamps must work well together visually. For example the small holly sprig border on the card shown here does not detract from the larger, simple, bold images of the dove and solid star. The solid star and outline dove create an interesting effect together. If those two stamps were not of similar size, the effect could be confusing, and certainly not as striking.

To ensure equal spacing when you wish to stamp several of the same image in a

Stamped holly sprigs create an interesting border.

row, stamp the first image in the middle, then stamp it on the ends and finally fill in the middle. A stamp positioner, ruler, or firm cardboard box with a straight edge helps to line up the stamps.

*W*hen stamping images over a large area (wrapping paper, for instance) one concern is that the images be spaced evenly. Use a grid to help you align and space the images. If you don't have a translucent cutting mat with a grid, prepare your own by drawing lines with a permanent marker on white paper or foam core. (Foam core works well because you can thumb tack your paper to it.) Lay your project over the grid and proceed.

*T*o create the illusion of depth, try stamping the image in the foreground first and then, without re-inking, stamp slightly higher on the page so that the images overlap.

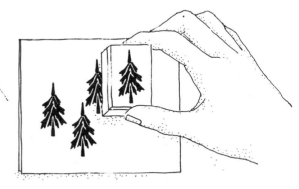

Stamped trees positioned to create depth.

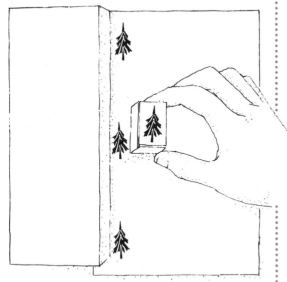

A straight edge helps when aligning multiple images.

MASKS

Stamping a scene is fun and easy to do. In fact, it is much less complicated than it looks. To create the illusion of depth in your scene, with one image appearing to be behind the other, use a simple masking technique. Begin by stamping on the paper the image that you want to appear closest to the viewer (in the foreground).

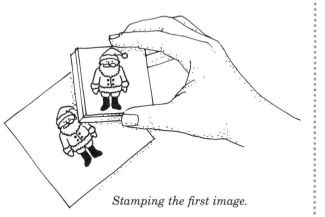

Stamping the first image.

Next, stamp that same image onto a piece of thin scrap paper, or a sticky note (a trade name for these gummed

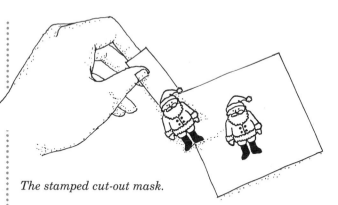

The stamped cut-out mask.

labels is Post-it). The sticky part of the note should be under your impression. If you don't have a sticky note handy, use scrap paper, but leave a "handle" to hold, as in the drawing here. Cut out the image carefully, staying just inside the outline. This is your mask. Place the mask over the already-stamped image to protect it. Now, stamp the second image (the one that you want to appear "behind" the first one) partly overlapping the first image.

You may have to increase the pressure applied on this stamp to compensate for the thickness of the mask and to prevent a gap between the two images. Remove the mask. You can repeat this process

Preparing to stamp over the mask.

over and over again on the same card to accentuate the illusion of depth.

*O*nce you have gone to the trouble to create this scene with masks you should certainly save the masks for future use. Maybe you plan to make 100 Christmas cards with this scene, or you might use the Santa figure alone in another scene. The mask can be used whenever you wish to use the Santa figure in combination with other stamps.

Store the masks you wish to keep in individual envelopes and be sure to mark the outside of each envelope by stamping the image on it. Or you might prefer to keep the envelopes in a notebook with acrylic pockets or pages.

Once the scene is completed, remove the mask.

*U*sing this same principle, you can cover a section of paper you want to keep clean and stamp the fully-inked image partially overlapping the mask. If you want just one of the presents from the *Stamp-A-Christmas*™ presents stamp to appear in your design, you could use this masking technique to block the other.

*T*o design a card with a Christmas stocking filled with the gingerbread man and candy cane, align a straight-edged piece of scrap paper with the top edge of the stocking. Stamp the images partially overlapping the mask. Remove the mask and the images will appear to be spilling out of the stocking. We used this technique to make the card shown here.

*Y*ou can also use a piece of paper as a mask to keep the back side of a folded card free of stamped images when you want to stamp right up to the folded edge. Open the card and place it on your work surface with the inside facing down. Cover the back side of the card with a piece of paper aligned at the fold,

and stamp the front of the card. Some of the images can spill over onto the mask. Remove the mask and you will have a straight edge.

*R*emember to open the card flat to stamp so that you have an even surface on which to work. If you try to stamp with the card folded, the ink will not take properly on the double edge.

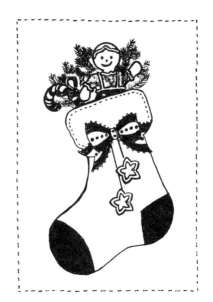

A filled-to-the-brim stocking.

FRAMES AND BORDERS

*F*rames and borders are attractive design elements that add an interesting dimension to your projects. Small stamps are particularly useful to create frames or borders on cards. There are many, many ways to create a frame or a border. For example, you might cut a shape out of paper and place it on top of your card stock. This is actually a

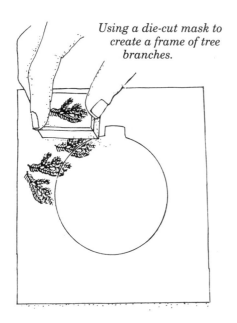

Using a die-cut mask to create a frame of tree branches.

mask. Stamp the images around the mask, allowing some to overlap the mask itself. This mask will be removed to leave a wonderful, clean-edged, framed space. You can vary the size and shape of the frame by changing the size and shape of the mask.

You probably have lots of ordinary things

Cutting a mortise mask.

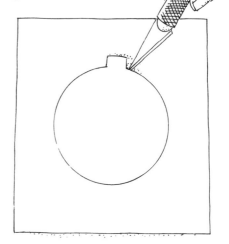

around the house that could be used to design masks. Index or playing cards will work well, for example. Or try tracing around cookie cutters or small containers to create masks of unusual shapes. You might want to try using the *Stamp-A-Christmas*™ die-cut tree ornaments as guides for cutting masks, as we did in the drawing on page 27.

To create a focal point and keep the frame of your card free of stamped images, prepare a "mortise mask"—a piece of paper the same size as your card with a shape or design cut out of the inside. Stamp the image inside the opening with some of the image falling on the mask that

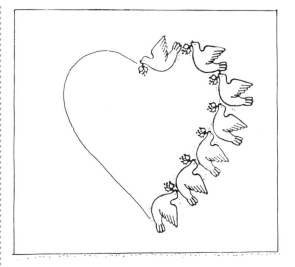

Repeating the dove stamp creates an appealing heart frame.

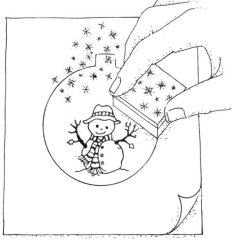

Using the mortise mask. The mask will be removed leaving a stamped scene in the ornament shape.

will be removed. When you remove the mortise mask, the shape will contain the stamped images, but the border of your card will be empty.

Another way to create a frame is to lightly pencil in a shape on your card and then stamp all along the penciled line so that the images create the shape you've drawn. After stamping, erase any pencil lines that show.

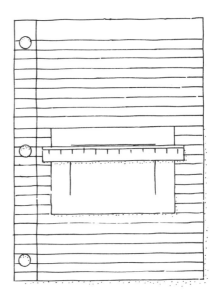

Connecting four corner images to create a frame.

card edge aligned with one of the rules on the paper. Using another rule of the paper as a guide for your ruler, draw a straight line across the card. If you want a frame on all four sides simply rotate the card and repeat. It might be best to draw the lines lightly in pencil so that any extra marks can be erased.

*Y*et another way to make a frame for your card is to stamp a small image in each of the four corners and then draw lines to connect each image. A simple border created by adding dots or dashes can also be very effective.

*A*n easy way to draw a straight line parallel to the edge of your card is to lay your card in the middle of a large sheet of ruled notebook paper, with the

Ruled paper used as guide for creating parallel lines.

3-D EFFECTS AND SHADOWS

*A*dd dimension to your work for a more realistic or whimsical effect. As you've learned, masking an image and stamping another image "behind" it gives the illusion of depth. This is only one of many techniques to achieve a three-dimensional look.

*W*hen you want an image to literally stand out from the others on the page, stamp it onto your card, then re-ink and stamp the image again on anoth-

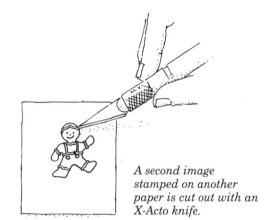

A second image stamped on another paper is cut out with an X-Acto knife.

er sheet of card stock. Cut out the image and apply a small piece of double-sided foam tape (available at stationery and office supply stores) to the back of the image. For a 3-D effect, position the cut-out image directly over the first image you stamped on the card. Use more layers of tape to achieve various heights in your overall design.

Stamping the image on a card. This image will become three-dimensional.

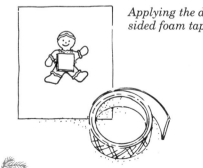

Applying the double-sided foam tape.

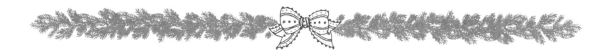

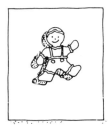

A three-dimensional gingerbread boy.

$\mathcal{F}$or another three-dimensional look, you can stamp an entire image on a card, and then, using an X-Acto knife, cut out part of it and bend the cut edges forward. This works best with a symmetrical design. For example, stamp the large angel included in the kit and cut around the outside of the wings (being careful to leave them attached to the body). Gently fold the wings forward.

$\mathcal{A}$nother way you can create depth in your design is to stamp an image in one color, and then stamp the same image in a second color 1/16 of an inch away (usually up and to one side). Don't forget to clean the stamp between inkings.

$\mathcal{T}$he addition of a shadow creates a dimension to your artwork. You can create a shadow by draw-ing a bold line along the outside edge of an image with markers. Determine where the light is coming from. This light source should affect each object in your design in the same way. Imagine the light source in the top right-hand corner of your paper. You would then add the shadow below and to the left of each image by drawing a line with a light gray, blue, or even lavender marker along the outer edge.

The angel's wings are cut and bent forward for a 3-D effect.

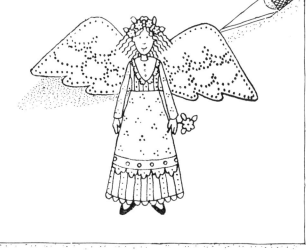

POP-UPS AND POP-OUTS

Pop-ups and pop-outs do just that. An image appears to jump out at you as you open the card, or extends beyond a folded edge of a card. Cards made using the following techniques are simple to execute but are guaranteed to surprise and please.

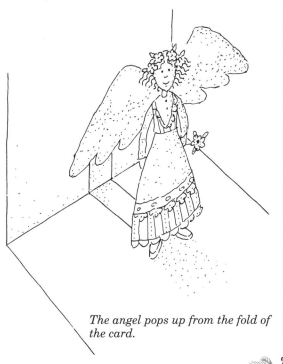

The angel pops up from the fold of the card.

Select a stamp that will fit within the dimensions of the card you are designing. In our kit the large angel was designed as a perfect pop-up image to be used with the cards in the kit. Stamp the image that will pop up from your card onto a separate card or index stock. Color the angel as you wish, and then carefully cut it out using a scissors or X-Acto knife. This cut-out image must be attached to a base to allow it to pop up when the card is opened.

To make the pop-up base, cut out a strip of card stock narrower than the pop-up image. To make our angel pop up, cut a base strip 4 inches long and 1/2 inch wide. Crease and fold the strip at one-inch increments. Open your card so that it lies flat, with the inside facing up. Decide at what horizontal point you want to place the pop-up image. Glue section 1 to the bottom of the card at that point, and section 4 to the top of the card so that the two ends of the strip meet at the fold of the card. Gently close the card to confirm that the measurements are accurate. Adjust the position as necessary. The cut-out angel will then be attached

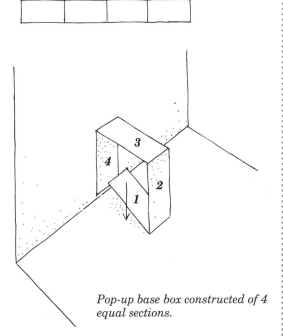

Pop-up base box constructed of 4 equal sections.

When selecting other pop-up images, you must be able to fit the stamped image plus the length of section 1 of the base within the height of the card. In our kit, the large angel is 2 1/2 inches high and segment 1 of the base is 1 inch. This total of 3 1/2 inches fits comfortably within the 4 1/4-inch height of our cards. If the pop-up image is too large it will protrude beyond the edges of the folded card and look unprofessional.

Here is another simple but intriguing pop-up card. With a card closed, measure along the fold, 2 inches from each side. At those two points, draw one-inch-long parallel lines down from the fold. These lines must be identical in length. Cut on the lines, fold the cut middle section over the front of the card and press down to crease. Turn the card over, fold the same section in the opposite direction, toward the back of the card. Open the card and press the middle, cut, piece up from behind to form a box shape or platform on which you will place your pop-up image. Close the card. The base will fold forward inside the card. Stamp the inside of the card

to side 2. The image lies flat when the card is closed and will automatically pop up when the card is opened.

This is one of the simplest ways to create a pop-up card. As you gain more experience creating pop-up cards you can experiment with different size bases.

and attach the image to the pop-up base. Carefully apply a thin layer of glue around the outside edges of the card. Open a second card and place the cut card inside the uncut card, matching the center folds. Press the two cards together; close the card gently, pulling the pop-up base toward you.

You need not be limited to one platform or base. You can make as many as you wish—a whole town's worth—and even pile one platform on top of another. And remember to experiment with scrap paper first.

You can learn about other methods by consulting any one of the many books on the subject that are available in the arts and crafts sections of most bookstores and libraries.

A pop-out card is similar to a pop-up, but the image can pop out from anywhere on your card. Unlike a pop-up image, a pop-out image does not have to be placed at the fold. Stamp the image that will pop out from the card onto card or index stock (sturdy paper). Color the image and cut it out. To construct a

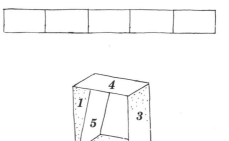

Pop-out base box constructed of 5 equal sections.

pop-out card, cut out a base similar to the one for pop-ups but with 5 equal parts instead of 4. Glue section 1 to section 5 to form a square box. Next, attach the already-glued together sections 1 and 5 to the card anywhere in your design. Glue your cut-out image to section 3. The pop-out image will lie flat when the card is closed. Once the card is opened, pop out the image by simply lifting it up.

Another kind of pop-out card is one in which the whole middle section of the card moves forward. This provides a wonderful viewmaster effect! To complete this project you need two cards of the same size.

the letter "M." Erase the pencil marks. This is now the inside of the card. At the center fold of the pop-out section, draw and cut out an area to view a scene. You will stamp the scene on the second card. In one of our projects (Number 98) we used the ball ornament as a cutting guide for the opening on the first card through which we see the snowman. Glue the two cards together, matching the edges. Gently close the card.

Pop-out base box is attached to the card.

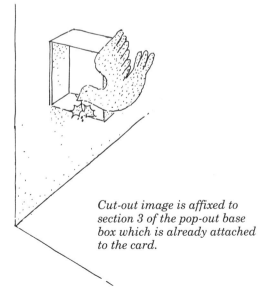

Cut-out image is affixed to section 3 of the pop-out base box which is already attached to the card.

$\mathscr{L}$ay one card flat with the outside facing up. Measure and draw a light pencil line 1 1/2 inches on either side of the center fold of the card. Each of the lines is parallel to the fold and runs across the width of the card. Score (make a slight indent) along the two pencil lines using a ruler and a bone folder, a large paper clip or a dull knife (actually anything that will crease but not break the paper surface). Gently fold the two outside sections forward at the scored lines. The card will be in the shape of

To make a card or placecard with an image that pops up above the fold-line, lay the paper or card flat and stamp part of the image—as much as half—above the fold-line. Using an X-Acto knife, cut around the part of the stamped image that is above the line. Score the card at the fold-line but do not score through the image. Fold the card, and the image will pop up.

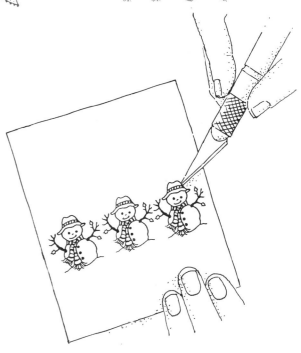

Part of the stamped image is above the fold of the card.

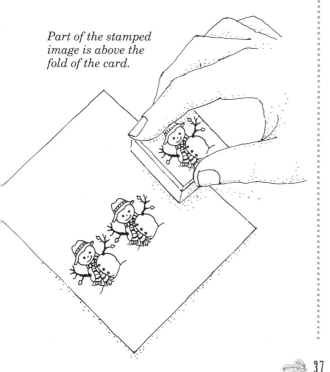

Cut out the portion of the image that is to extend beyond the fold.

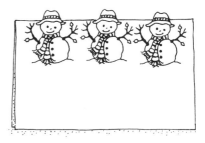

Fold the card, and the image pops-up above the fold.

THE ILLUSION OF MOTION

$\mathscr{I}$f you want to make an image appear to be moving, first ink your stamp and stamp it on the paper. Lift the stamp off of the paper and, without re-inking it, re-stamp only the "trailing" portion of the design several times, close together and in the direction from which you wish the image to appear to be coming.

$\mathscr{A}$nother way to show movement is to stamp the image and, without re-inking or lifting the stamp, drag it backwards. You may want to try this with the angel stamp to make her appear to be flying.

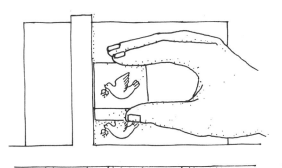

Place the stamp in the angle of the stamp positioner to align images on the page.

THE STAMP POSITIONER

$\mathscr{W}$e have used a wonderful tool in making the projects for this kit. Although it is not included in the kit, we do recommend it. A stamp positioner is not essential, but it is helpful in aligning images on the page. It is perfect for making masks, borders, and correcting mistakes. Stamp an image on tissue paper, using the positioner as a guide; remove the tissue paper and stamp the image on your card in the correct spot.

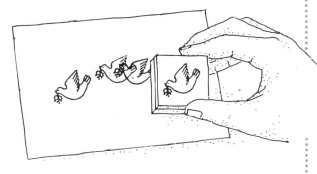

A flock of doves moves across the page.

NEW TECHNIQUES AND MATERIALS

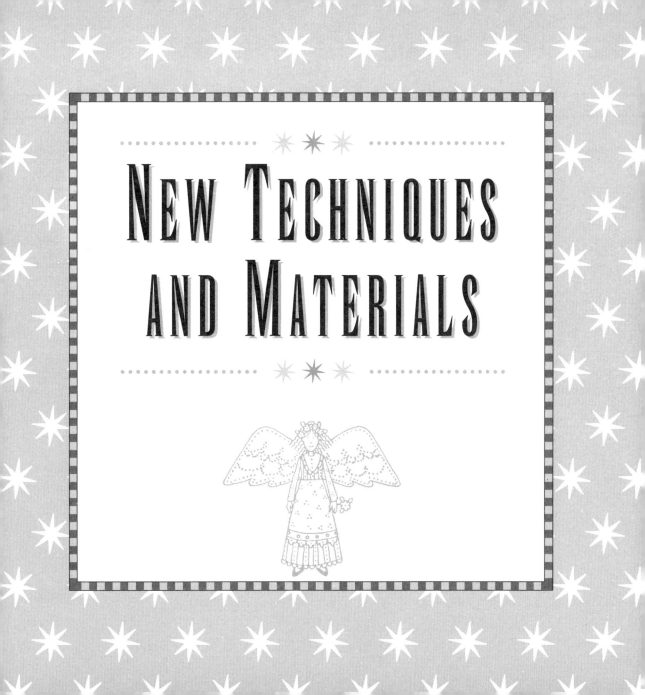

Moving On

*N*ow that you have read the section on the basics of stamping and completed many projects using the *Stamp-A-Christmas*™ kit, you know how easy it is to express yourself with the basic products and instructions for stamping.

*Y*ou are ready to move on to more advanced techniques.

*Y*our stamped artwork can be embellished with many different design elements using a variety of art materials. This section introduces you to many of those materials and the techniques you need to know to use them. But before starting you might review this suggested list of additional materials—all of which are readily available at rubber stamp stores and many craft and art supply stores across the country. The Great American Stamp Store is also a full service source for all your stamping supplies.

* Pigment ink
* Embossing powders
* Embossing pens
* Heat gun
* Rainbow ink pads
* Paper - vellum, rag, watercolor, tissue.
* Ribbon
* Crack and Peel (sticker) paper
* Watercolor pencils and brushes
* Soft chalks
* Sponges
* Brayer
* Eraser (or reverse-image stamp)
* Glitter (various colors)
* Glue stick
* Foam brushes
* Acrylic paints (for wood), sand paper
* Spray acrylic sealer
* Paper cutter, deckle scissors

PIGMENT INKS

Pigment ink, available in pads of many different sizes and shapes, is opaque, unlike dye-based ink. This means that the color of your paper will not affect the color of the ink.

Pigment ink is available in a wide range of colors, including many metallic shades like gold, silver, and copper. Pigment ink resists fading and has a balanced pH, which minimizes acid deterioration. Consequently, it is an ideal choice to use in combination with other artwork or photographs. Pigment ink is slow-drying, and requires an absorbent surface. However, if you want to use it to stamp on glossy or coated paper (which is nonabsorbent), you must emboss the ink to make it permanent. It is this slow-drying quality that makes pigment ink ideal to use when embossing on any paper (see page 45).

To ensure an even ink coverage, the best way to ink your stamp with a pigment pad is to hold the stamp in one hand with the rubber image facing up and gently pat the entire stamp with the ink pad,

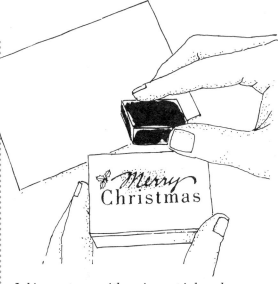

Inking a stamp with a pigment ink pad.

held in the other hand. Hold the stamp at an angle in the light to determine if there are any dry spots. If the stamp does not appear to be entirely wet, tap the stamp with the ink pad again. This method of inking allows you to cover even the largest stamp with a small ink pad.

Be careful not to over-ink your stamp when applying pigment ink. Because this ink is thick, over-inking will fill in the recessed areas of the stamp and make it difficult to get a clear, detailed impression, or cause an undesirable shadow.

RAINBOW INK PADS

*R*ainbow ink pads contain three or more colors or shades of the same color. They are available in both pigment and dye ink. Using rainbow ink pads is a very simple way to add variety to your stamped art.

*T*here are two methods of manufacturing dye rainbow pads. The less expensive pad is created by cutting the felt pad into strips or sections and applying a different color to each section. These pads separate the colors with plastic dividers which must be removed before use. After stamping with such a pad you may be able to see the separations on your finished artwork, especially if you use a design with a lot of solid area. To compensate for the separations, you may want to move the stamp around slightly as you tap it onto the ink pad. This ensures an even coverage of ink over the entire surface of the stamp. Other rainbow pads are made by hand with the application of the ink to the felt. The colors blend well as the inks flow together. Over time the ink on all types of dye-based rainbow pads flows together, modifying the colors. To slow this process it is important to clean your stamp before use and after each impression, and always store the pad flat. Dye rainbow pads can produce dazzling results, especially on glossy or coated paper. Try using a brayer with rainbow pads to create great backgrounds.

*T*here are also multicolored pigment ink pads that will give results similar to those of the dye-based rainbow pads. Because of the inherent properties of pigment ink the colors will never blend together on the foam pad. Tapping your stamp several times with different areas of the pad will produce a kaleidoscopic effect. If mixing the colors on your stamp has carried one color onto the top of another on the pad, restore your pad to its original color by simply wiping it vertically with a clean, dry paper towel. Both pigment and dye inks are available in bottles so that you can re-ink your pads when they dry out. You can also use these bottled inks to make your own rainbow pads out of an un-inked felt or foam stamp pad.

OTHER INKS

Many types of paints and inks can be used to stamp images. We have used both poster and acrylic paint and metallic pens. If the ink or paint is water-based, try it. Be sure to clean your stamp thoroughly immediately after use. Some office ink pads contain chemicals that could dry out the rubber of your stamps and should not be used.

PAPERS

A wonderful and easy way to add new dimension to your stamping projects is to use a variety of papers. Many colors, textures, and weights are available.

The paper included in your kit—an uncoated white stock—is easy to use and will accept all types of ink. Experiment with a few sheets before buying paper in bulk. Each kind of paper responds in its own way to ink.

To achieve the brightest colors when using dye-based inks or pens, select a glossy or coated paper. Coated paper tends to be slippery, so be sure to hold the paper down with one hand as you lift your stamp with the other. Pigment inks need matte paper. The absorbing qualities allow the pigment ink to dry. Some papers called "matte" are in fact "matte coated," and will not work with pigment ink unless the pigment-inked image is embossed.

Many specialty papers are available. Some are marbled or metallic; some are made by hand; some incorporate glitter or are gummed on the back so that you can make stickers with them. Your mailbox is a great paper source. Magazines, advertisements, and junk mail often contain great designs and unusual papers. Recycle whenever possible.

Sticker-backed paper is available in matte or glossy finish and has the same ink requirements as regular matte or glossy-finished paper. After stamping on sticker paper, cut out the image and apply it to your artwork for a layered look. As your stamping experience grows, your awareness of new and interesting raw materials will develop. Printed cards and invitations often carry blank areas that can be used in new creations.

EMBOSSING WITH INK

*E*mbossing involves heat-treating a print of a stamp to create a raised, shiny, or metallic impression. It is a stunning, professional looking technique that you will want to explore as your stamping abilities grow.

*E*mbossing can be used to make a durable impression on all types of paper as well as on many other surfaces, such as plastic, glass, fabric, and wood. Embossed images are permanent. They do not fade with heat, light, or time.

*P*igment inks are best to use for embossing because of their slow-drying qualities. Embossing fluid, both clear and tinted, is available in a pad or dauber-top bottle. There are embossing pens with fine, calligraphic, and brush tips.

*Y*ou can use glue sticks to emboss stunning borders, hand-drawn designs, or written greetings. The best glue stick to use is one containing liquid glue in a pen form. These are available with various writing tips.

*M*any different types of embossing powders are available, and each produces a different effect. Clear embossing powder enhances the color of the ink, making it raised and shiny. Metallic and colored embossing powders will cover the ink, and tinsel powders will add sparkle. Pearl, iridescent, and psychedelic powders may modify the color of the ink used. Texture powders can give you the look and feel of cement or terra cotta. These are just a few examples of the powders currently available. New embossing powders are being introduced regularly.

*Y*ou need a heat source of at least 300 degrees Fahrenheit to melt the embossing powder applied to your stamped image. The heat sources most commonly used for embossing are heat guns, toasters, an iron set on "cotton," an electric stove top, and an oven set at 300 degrees Fahrenheit. The commercially available "Craft Heat Gun" is the easiest and most efficient tool to use because of its steady and even heat flow. It resembles a hand-held hair dryer. Unfortunately, standard hair dryers do not get hot enough to use for embossing.

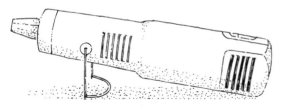

A heat gun—the most efficient tool to use for embossing.

THE EMBOSSING PROCESS

*A*pply pigment ink or embossing fluid to the stamp and stamp the image on the paper. While the ink is still wet, pour embossing powder generously over the image. Make sure your hands are dry and clean because the oils from your

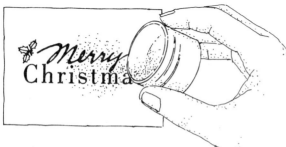

Sprinkling embossing powder on a stamped image.

hands may transfer to the paper and catch embossing powder.

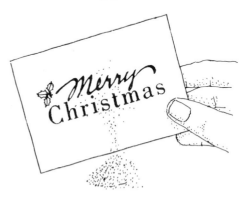

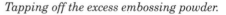

Tapping off the excess embossing powder.

*T*ilt the paper and tap off excess powder. The powder will adhere to the stamped image. Use a clean, dry, soft paint brush to brush away any powder that sticks to areas other than the image. If you accidentally brush powder off your stamped image, reapply the powder, while ink is still wet. If you buy several jars of each of your favorite embossing powders to pour into plastic food containers, you have the option of dipping your cards in the container for faster application. The plastic containers also work well to catch the unused powder.

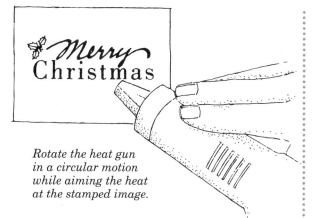

Rotate the heat gun in a circular motion while aiming the heat at the stamped image.

$\mathcal{H}$old the heat gun about 4 to 6 inches from the stamped image to melt the embossing powder. Apply the hot air in a circular motion until the entire image is embossed. You will see the powder melt and become shiny. If you are using alternate sources of heat, such as the iron, toaster, or stove top, move the paper in a slow circular motion, applying the heat to the underside. Continue heating just long enough for the powder to melt. (Of course, adult supervision is required whenever children are using any of these heat sources.)

$\mathcal{T}$he following tips should help you become adept at embossing.

❋ Be careful not to overheat the powder. Overheating may flatten out and dull the embossed image and/or scorch your paper.

❋ To avoid smudges, do not touch the embossed image while it is still hot. Let it cool and harden before touching it.

❋ Use a clothespin or tongs to hold the paper and to keep your fingers away from the heat source.

❋ An embossing pen can be used as a correction tool. Draw in areas that did not emboss, reapply powder, and heat.

❋ When you are embossing several cards at the same time, you can stamp and apply the powder to all of the cards before applying the heat source.

❋ If you find that the paper warps from the heat, let it cool and then flatten it by placing it under a book or heavy object. Let it sit for at least an hour.

SPECIAL EMBOSSING TECHNIQUES

*Y*ou can use an embossing pen or brush tip embossing marker to highlight or fill in areas of specific stamped images. This can be done immediately after embossing an image. However, if your images have not been embossed, wait until the ink has dried completely before using the pen. Metallic or colored embossing powders will cover the color of your paper or stamped image. You may want to add silver ornaments to a tree or wreath by drawing them in with the embossing pen and then embossing the images with silver powder. Or you might want to decorate an open star by filling it in with the embossing pen and then using gold powder.

MULTIPLE POWDERS ON ONE IMAGE

*T*o achieve an unusual effect, use various colors of embossing powder on the same image. Start by inking the entire stamp with one shade of pigment ink or embossing fluid. Sprinkle the desired embossing powders, one at a time, on specific sections of the image, tapping off the excess powder before applying the next color. Heat the embossing powder only after all the colors have been applied. This technique works best with metallic powders on solid images. Try using gold, silver, and copper on a leaf or a sun for a sensational effect.

EMBOSSING A FRAME OR BORDER

*F*or a thin, uneven border, hold the card upright and pull the edge through pigment ink or embossing fluid. Dip the card into the embossing powder and heat. For a wider border, try using a chiseled-point glue stick. Lay the card stock on your work surface. Using the edge of the card as your guide, run the glue stick along the edge to the desired thickness. In creating both types of borders, emboss only two edges at a time. This will allow you to hold the card while heating it without transferring the powders to areas you don't want to emboss. A third method to use for embossing a frame or border is to place double-sided cellophane tape on the area you want to emboss. Be sure all sections of the the tape are securely attached to your paper before applying the embossing powder. Heat as instructed above.

To make a more whimsical frame for a stamped image, use an embossing pen to draw a line, dots, or dashes around it, using a ruler or template as a guide. If you make a mistake, remember that embossing pens are erasable. Try stamping an image in each corner of your card and using the embossing pen to connect them. This technique is great for framing an address on an envelope, or names on place cards or name tags.

DOUBLE EMBOSSING

The technique of double embossing works best for a stamped design that will be colored in. Start by embossing the image as you would normally, using the embossing powder of your choice. Color the image using markers or colored pencils. Using the brush-tip embossing pen or clear embossing fluid on a brush, paint a thin layer over the entire image, and sprinkle with clear embossing powder. Tap off excess powder, and heat for a dazzling enameled or stained glass effect.

ADDING COLOR TO YOUR DESIGN

WATERCOLOR PENCILS

When watercolor pencils are wet, the colors run like paint. They can give your artwork the look of a watercolor painting. First, choose a stamp that has large open areas to fill in with color. Stamp the image using permanent ink, or emboss it to make it permanent.

Experiment with the following methods to add interesting color to your projects:

✳ Color in the image with your watercolor pencil, just as you would with markers or regular colored pencils. Then use a clean brush or a fine-mist spray bottle to apply a small amount of water and blend the colors.

✳ To create more intense colors wet your paper and draw with dry watercolor pencils.

✳ Dip the pencil in water and draw directly on either wet or dry paper. This method produces the strongest color.

* You can also remove pigment from the tip of the pencil using a moistened brush and then transfer it to your stamped image, as in traditional water-color painting. When you want to mix colors, create a palette on a separate piece of paper and blend the colors together with a wet brush. Apply the desired color to your stamped image with a brush.

*Y*ou may find that your paper curls when wet, but it should flatten back out as it dries. If it does not dry flat, place the paper between heavy books overnight.

WATER-BASED PAINT

*W*atercolor paint can be used in the same manner as watercolor pencils. You can use pigment ink pads or pigment re-inkers as a color source. Lightly moisten your brush with a small amount of tap water. Brush the slightly moistened paint brush over the pigment ink. Apply the color directly to your stamped design. Dip the brush into water if the ink starts to dry. Repeat the process with all the other colors until your entire design is complete.

SOFT CHALKS

*C*halks create soft, light colors. They are available pressed into squares or sticks and can be used on almost any paper stock. Apply chalk sticks as you would any crayon or pencil. Chalk squares can be applied with your fingers, cotton swabs, sponges, etc.

Brushing a small amount of water to blend the colors on the stamped image.

BLEACH

*T*ry creating "negative" images by using bleach instead of ink. Create a pad by soaking a piece of sponge or felt in bleach. Stamp on dark paper and watch as the faded images appear. The shades of bleaching will vary depending upon the color and quality of paper used.

APPLYING GLITTER

*A*n alternative to using the glitter glue you received in this kit is to use glitter and a glue stick separately. The glue stick will dry faster and is easier to control. Use glitter in many of the same ways as you would embossing powder, to create frames or borders on your cards. Glitter is available in a variety of colors and textures.

CREATING BACKGROUNDS

SPONGING

*Y*ou can fashion a variety of backgrounds for stamped art, including an air-brushed effect, by using sponges. It is the texture of the sponge that gives the effect. Cosmetic, porous household and natural sponges will all work. Cosmetic sponges create a soft look, while the porous household sponge gives a mottled

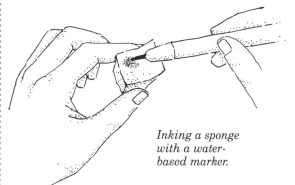

Inking a sponge with a water-based marker.

appearance. A background made with a natural sponge will appear lacy. There are sponges specifically designed for the purpose of creating backgrounds— some are even on rollers. Look for these products at your local rubber stamp or craft store.

*S*tart with a dry sponge and color it with a water-based marker. If your sponge does not have round edges, gather the whole sponge up in your fingertips to prevent edges from showing.

$\mathcal{B}$lot the sponge on scrap paper to remove any excess ink and then tap it lightly all over your paper to create a soft background. For convenience, you may want to have several sponges on hand, reserving one for each color. Wash out your sponges when you are finished with a project. Experiment with mixing colors on your paper. For example, you can suggest a beautiful sunset by lightly layering pink over a blue sky.

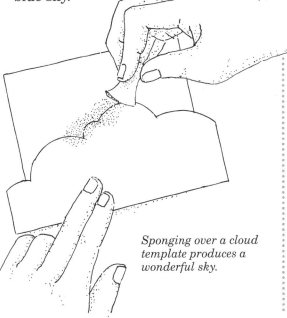

Sponging over a cloud template produces a wonderful sky.

$\mathcal{Y}$ou may also apply color by tapping the sponge onto an ink pad or into any other water-based ink or paint. Metallic paints give a dazzling effect to any background. Sponging over a stencil or mask of any shape is another option. Try cutting a piece of paper into the shape of a cloud. Sponge over the edge of your cloud stencil. For an overall cloudy sky, repeat the sponging, moving the stencil around on your paper. Try making patterned backgrounds by sponging over netting, a paper doily, or lace. Use sponging to fill in or to give depth to stamped grass, sand, or water.

$\mathcal{T}$ry this sponging technique using all types of paper—paper towels, tissue paper, or facial tissues—to provide some interesting textures. Scrunch up the material in your fingers, ink it , and then tap it lightly on your paper. Each paper will produce a different effect.

SPATTERING

$\mathcal{S}$prinkle your design with dots of color by spattering ink onto the paper with a toothbrush. Use the ink available to refill pigment ink pads, or acrylic paint. Water

bristles spring forward and spatter the medium onto the surface. The more paint you have on your brush, the larger the dots will be. With less paint on the brush, the dots become smaller.

Spattering would create a wonderful background for the angel stamp or the snowman.

USING A BRAYER

A brayer is a small paint roller made out of rubber. It was originally designed for linoleum block printing, but it is another great tool to use with stamping. Use it to apply ink to the surface of your stamp or directly to the paper. Brayers are available in many widths, and work well with both pigment and dye-based inks. They are the best tools available for applying a smooth background color to a paper surface.

To start, cover the entire roller surface with ink, using short, sweeping strokes over the ink pad. Next, roll the brayer evenly over the paper or card in a continuous back-and-forth motion. Repeating this process will intensify

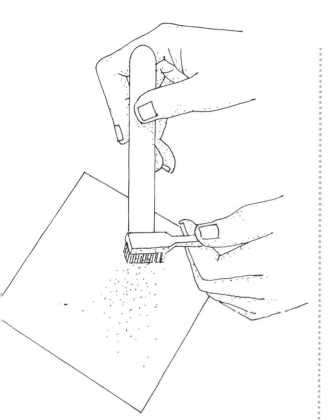

Creating a snowy background is easy using an old toothbrush to spatter the ink.

down the medium before dipping in the toothbrush. While holding the toothbrush over your paper, draw a knife or ice cream stick across the brush, causing the bristles to bend. As you release, the

the color. Always keep scrap paper under your work so that you can roll off the edge of your artwork. Rainbow stamp pads work well for this process. With them you can create an instant sunset or beautiful background for any creation. Clean your brayer just as you would your rubber stamps.

TRY USING THE BRAYER IN THE FOLLOWING WAYS:

✳ Apply color on paper and then stamp an outlined image over the color. Cut out the image and add it to your artwork. If you have used card stock, this will give a 3-D effect. Done on sticker paper, it will offer a layered look.

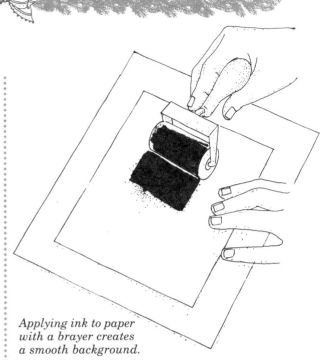

Applying ink to paper with a brayer creates a smooth background.

✳ Obtain a "batik" effect by using wax or crayons with the brayer. First, draw a design on your paper with a waxy crayon. Then apply ink over the entire surface using the brayer. The wax from the crayon will resist ink from the brayer.

✳ Create plaids by applying different inks to your paper with small brayers, then crisscrossing horizontal and vertical stripes.

✳ Use water-based markers to draw designs directly onto the brayer. Then transfer those designs to your paper with the brayer.

✳ Ink large stamps by rolling the brayer on the ink pad and then over the stamp.

ROLLER STAMPS

Specially designed roller stamps can be used in many of the same ways as the brayer. Some are even self-inking, which is terrific when you need to cover large surfaces quickly.

REVERSING AN IMAGE

*W*hen you want an image on a stamp to face in the opposite direction, use the technique called reversing. Stamp gently onto a flat rubber surface, such as a large eraser, with pigment ink. (Pressing too hard may cause the ink to spread on the rubber.) While the ink is still wet, stamp the eraser onto your artwork, using extra pressure. This reverse image will be lighter in color than an initial stamping using the same ink. Therefore, if you want to print the original next to the reversed image for a mirrored effect, stamp the reversed image first and then, without re-ink-

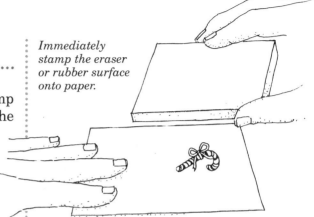

Immediately stamp the eraser or rubber surface onto paper.

ing the stamp, press it onto your paper. It is important to clean the flat rubber surface immediately after stamping. Use a damp paper towel and clean it in the same way as you clean your stamps. Flat, rubber-surfaced stamps designed specifically for reversing an image are available.

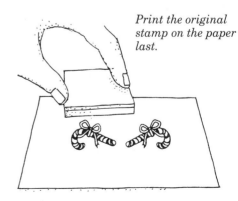

Print the original stamp on the paper last.

Stamp onto a flat rubber surface using pigment ink.

FABRIC STAMPING

*R*ubber stamping on fabric is a great way to personalize clothing, add dazzle to your plain napkins for the holidays, and make unique gifts. You can use almost any fabric but those with smooth textures work best.

*B*efore you begin, wash the fabric to remove any sizing, but do not use fabric softeners. Iron the fabric to remove wrinkles. You may find it helpful to use an embroidery hoop to support a delicate fabric while stamping. Because the ink may bleed through the fabric, put a piece of cardboard under it before you begin. If you are working on a T-shirt, put the cardboard between the front and back of the shirt.

*I*f you are printing on a loosely knit fabric, bond freezer paper onto the wrong side of the garment to hold the fabric firm, keep it from stretching, and also prevent the ink from bleeding through to the back of the garment. To bond freezer paper to the fabric press the paper shiny side down with an iron set for synthetics. When your project is finished, simply pull off the paper.

*W*hen you are working on a knit garment that will be stretched when worn such as leggings or tights, you must stretch the fabric before stamping to avoid having a distorted image. Turn the garment inside out and stretch it to the same degree that it will be stretched when worn. To keep the fabric stretched while you work, attach self-adhesive packing tape where you want to stamp the designs. Turn the garment right side out. After stamping, pull the tape off and the fabric will return to its original shape.

Applying fabric paint to a rubber stamp with a small foam brush.

PERMANENT INKS

Permanent ink dries quickly and does not wash out. You must use a solvent-based cleaner to remove this ink from your stamps. Permanent ink is available in a dauber-topped bottle. Use the dauber to apply the ink directly to the stamp and then stamp onto your fabric. With this product, it is possible to apply several colors to one stamp at the same time. Permanent fabric inks are also available in stamp pads which are useful for repetitive stamping of the same color. Because fabric inks dry quickly, a fabric pad will require re-inking often.

FABRIC PAINTS

Fabric paints come in a wide range of colors. The easiest way to apply fabric paint to a stamp is to use inexpensive foam brushes, sold at any paint store. Keep a supply of cotton swabs handy to clean any area of the stamp that may pick up excess paint before stamping. Because most fabric paints do not become permanent until they dry, you can clean your stamps and brushes with water while the paint is still wet.

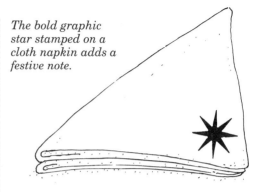

The bold graphic star stamped on a cloth napkin adds a festive note.

TRANSFER INK

Transfer ink allows you to stamp a design on paper and then use an iron to transfer the design to fabric. These inks are available in pads of various colors and will work on any paper. When you are happy with the images you stamped on paper, simply iron them on the fabric as directed. This ink works best on fabric that is smooth and contains some polyester.

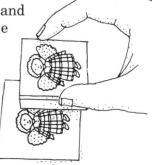

Stamping on transfer-inked paper.

Ironing a transfer onto an already-ironed T-shirt sleeve.

Don't forget that when you use a transfer process you will end up with a mirror image of the original design so this technique will not work with words.

The finished product—a one-of-a-kind T-shirt!

EMBOSSED PIGMENT INK

*Y*ou can emboss any pigment ink on fabric to make it permanent. Smooth-surfaced fabrics work best, because it is easier to remove any excess embossing powder from them before heating. Use the same heat sources for fabric as you use for paper.

*T*he type of fabric and the method you choose will both affect the results. Therefore, always test the stamps and ink on a scrap of your fabric before beginning your project. When you want to color in an outlined image, be sure to use pens designed for fabric.

*Y*ou may want to embellish your stamped designs by using fabric puff-paint and glitter pens designed to be permanent when applied to fabric. Use glue designed for fabric to affix rhinestones and trinkets. Try making Christmas stockings or ornaments using plain fabric and your favorite Christmas stamps.

STAMPING ON WOOD AND OTHER SURFACES

*I*nexpensive, unfinished wood products can be purchased at craft stores and decorated using rubber stamps. Before stamping, sand the wood to create a smooth surface. You may also decide to stain the wood before starting. Plan your design keeping in mind that small images are easier to stamp on curved surfaces.

*U*se pigment ink or acrylic paint and test your colors on a similar type of wood, as they may produce different shades on various woods. Stamp the design and let the ink dry thoroughly before adding additional color. You can emboss on wood to add a metallic or shiny finish to your design using the same techniques as for paper. (Of course, the heat has to be applied from above.)

*A*ny object that requires washing should be given a protective finish after stamping. We recommend using a spray varnish because applying a fixative with a brush may cause the paint to run.

*T*he same process that is used to stamp and emboss on wood also works well on papier-mache boxes. A stamped recipe box with matching stamped recipe cards makes a wonderful gift. You might even add some of your favorite holiday recipes. A stamped picture frame surrounding your favorite angel makes a great gift for Grandma.

*Y*our stamps will work on glass, metal, ceramics, or hard acrylic surfaces if you use pigment ink and embossing powder to make the image permanent. Glass stains or paints are available if you wish to add color to your designs.

*Y*ou could use this technique to print the star stamp in your kit onto a glass Christmas ornament, or to decorate a gift box to hold your favorite cookies or holiday treats.

*C*lay pots can also be decorated with stamps. After wiping the pot to remove any dust, spray the outside with clear acrylic spray and let it dry. Plan your design and use fabric ink or fabric paint to stamp the pot. When the ink is dry, seal it with acrylic spray. Insert a plastic pot into the clay pot before using it for live plants. Clay pots are also fun to use as unique gift baskets or to hold flowering bulbs like amaryllis or narcissus.

SPECIAL TREE ORNAMENTS

*W*ith your *Stamp-A-Christmas*™ kit and a few additional supplies, you can make tree ornaments that will be cherished for years. Start with a basic round shape—a circle or oval. A round- or egg-shaped ornament would work well. You could also use a real egg as the base. If you want to use a real egg, however, you will want to remove the inside, otherwise it will spoil. Carefully poke a small hole in one end and break the egg sack with a toothpick or a straight pin. Poke a pin hole in the opposite end, and gently blow out the white and yolk of the egg. Rinse out the egg with warm water, and then let it dry.

*S*ponge an all-over background design on the dry egg with paint or ink. Stamp the images you want to put on the egg onto tissue paper using pigment ink. Emboss the images and then color the reverse side of the image with fabric ink, water-based markers, colored pencils, or crayons. You've stamped and embossed the front and then colored the back (to prevent possible bleeding when glue is applied).

*C*ut out the images and apply them to the egg, using a white glue that becomes clear as it dries. Or you might want to use any of the special products designed especially for decoupage.

*I*f you colored the stamped, embossed image with water-based markers, be careful when applying the glue to prevent it from bleeding through to the other side. If you colored the back side of the images this shouldn't be a problem. However, just to be safe, it is best to lightly dab the first coat of glue instead of brushing across the design. Place the designs on the egg with the embossed sides facing out.

*T*o finish the ornament, apply several thin coats of glue, waiting at least 15 minutes between coats. Lightly sand between each coat with number 400 wet or dry sandpaper. If desired, a clear acrylic sealer can be applied over the glue. Decorate the ornament with pearls, jewels, or ribbon to cover the holes made for blowing out the inside of the egg. A glue gun is useful for applying this trim.

MOUNTING STAMPS

*A*s you work with the stamps from your kit you may decide you'd like to mount them onto wood blocks. This is very easy to do. First, you need a cushion between the rubber die and the mount. There are cushions designed specifically for rubber-stamp mounting, but you can also use craft foam, or even foam shoe inserts. For mounts, consider scraps of wood, wooden blocks, plastic boxes, empty thread spools, or empty jars. To begin, firmly pull the rubber die from the foam mounting and trim the die using scissors. Cut close to the design, but be careful not to undercut the image. Use rubber cement to mount the stamp to the cushion. Once the glue has set, cut the cushion to the same size or slightly larg-er than the die. Then, again using rubber cement, attach the cushion and stamp to your mount. Be sure that the die is parallel to the straight edge of the mount.

*Y*ou can print a label, or index, on the back of a wooden block by stamping the image onto the wood using pigment ink or permanent ink. You can also index the stamp by stamping on a piece of paper and attaching that to the block with heavy-duty clear tape. For accuracy in printing, it is important to place the index of your stamp in the same position on the top of your block as the die is on the bottom.

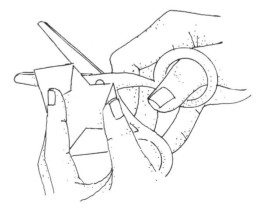

Trimming a rubber die to mount onto the wooden block.

MAKING A STAMP

To create a simple design, such as a solid heart or star, cut the shape out of foam. It is easy to cut with scissors and is self-adhesive so that you can apply it to a hard surface before stamping. Compressed sponge, another material used for stamp-making, is also easy to work with. Draw your design on the sponge and cut it out. Then wet the sponge to expand its thickness. It is easier to stamp a sponge if you mount it first onto a hard surface using rubber cement. Mounting the sponge also helps keep your hands clean. Fun craft punches in many shapes and sizes can be used to punch shapes out of the sponge. Both the foam and the sponge can be used with any ink. You can purchase foam specially designed for making stamps at most rubber stamp and craft stores.

CARVING A STAMP

To create a stamp with a lot of detail, use carving tools and large flat erasers. Draw directly onto an eraser keeping in mind that the image you stamp will be the reverse of what you carve.

Another option is to draw onto tracing paper using a soft lead pencil. Blacken the portions of the design that you want to print. Place the design face down on the eraser and firmly rub across the back of the paper with a blunt object to transfer the pencil drawing from the paper onto your eraser. This is the easiest way to carve words. Cut away the unmarked portions of the eraser. Use tools made for linoleum carving or any other small craft knives to cut the rubber. For safety, cut away from yourself. Make cuts at least 1/8 inch deep.

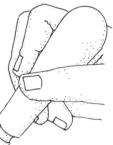

Carving a stamp of your own design is very rewarding.

Stamp-a-Christmas Special™ Projects

If you have read this far, you have all the information you need to complete the projects shown in full color on the next pages. Instructions for completing these projects follow the color pages. These projects have been planned to jump-start your creativity. You may choose to follow these instructions precisely just like a recipe and recreate these projects for yourself, or just use them as inspiration—a source book of ideas—for your own creations.

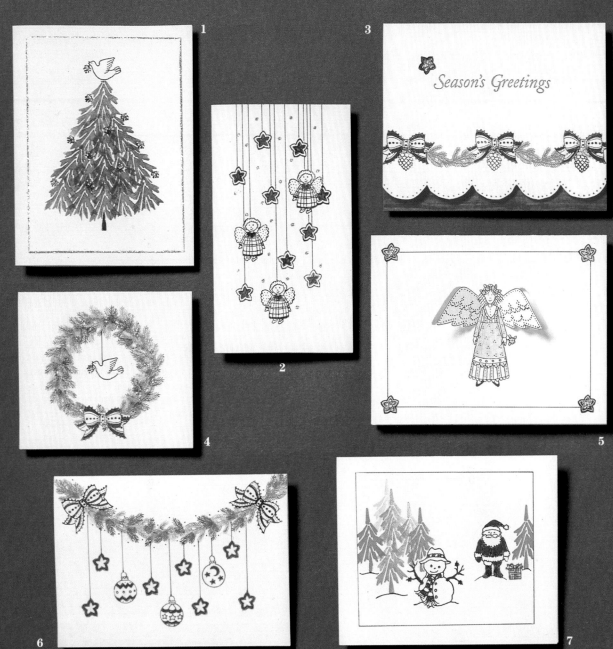

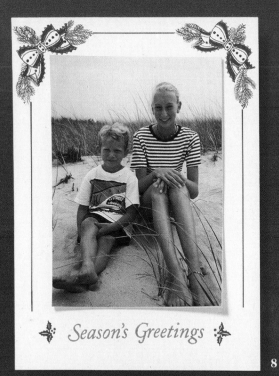

Season's Greetings

8

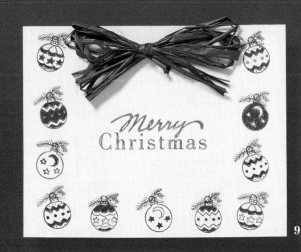

Merry Christmas

9

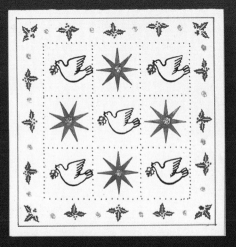

10

11

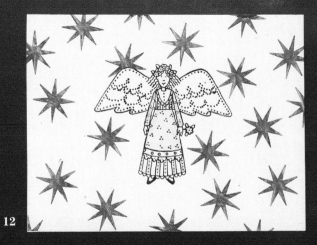

12

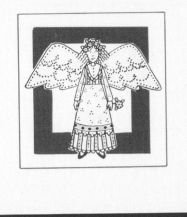

13

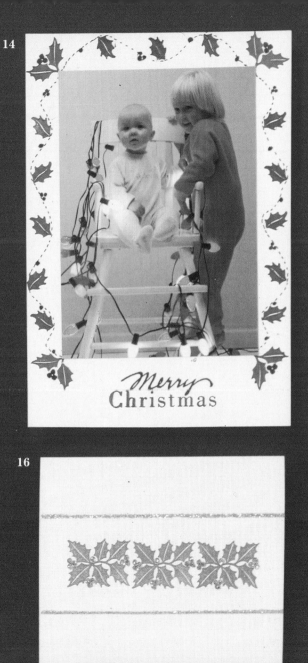

14

Merry Christmas

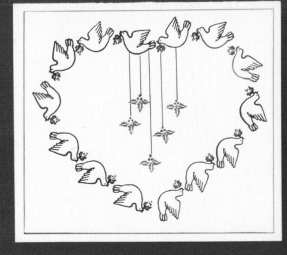

15

16

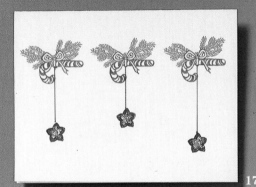

17

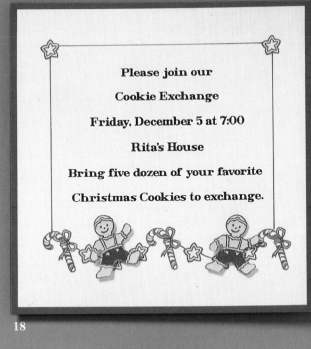

Please join our

Cookie Exchange

Friday, December 5 at 7:00

Rita's House

Bring five dozen of your favorite

Christmas Cookies to exchange.

18

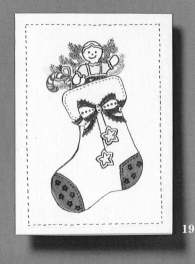

19

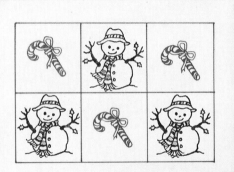

20

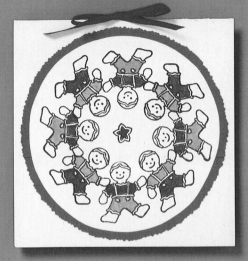

21

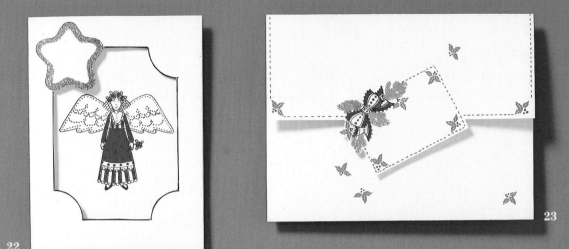

22

23

24

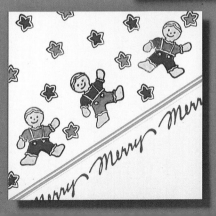

25

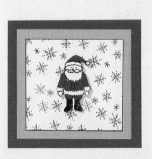

26

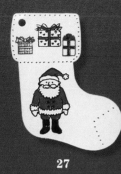

27

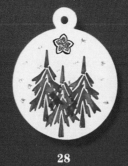

28

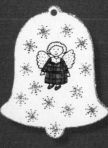

29

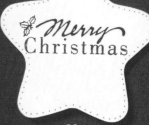

Merry Christmas

30

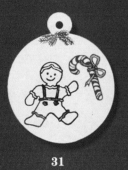

31

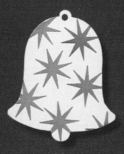

32

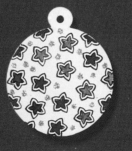

33

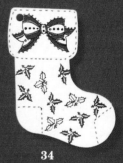

34

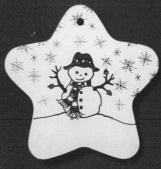

35

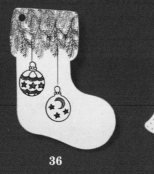

36

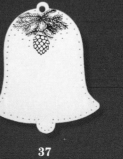

37

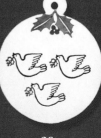

38

39

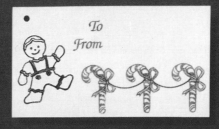

40

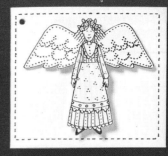

41

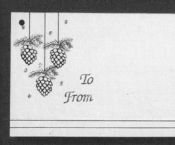

42

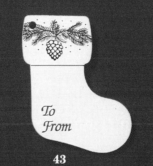

43

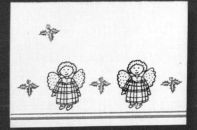

44

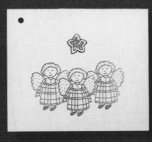

45

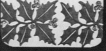

46

47

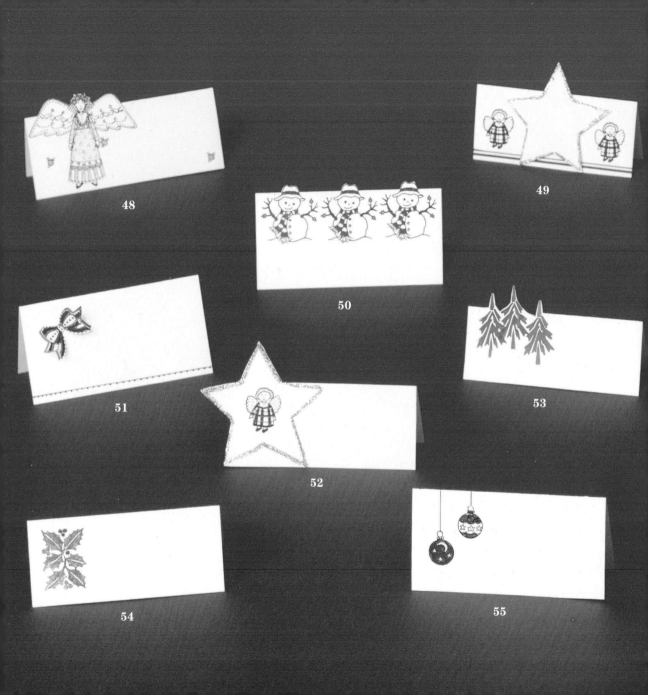

48

49

50

51

52

53

54

55

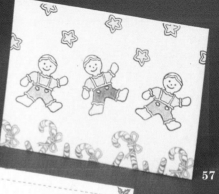

56

57

58

59

Grandma's Molasses Cookies

1 cup sugar
1 cup morgerine
2 eggs
1 cup molasses
4 tsp. baking soda
1/2 cup sour milk

3/4 tsp. salt
1 tblsp. cinnamon
1 tsp. ginger
1 tsp. cloves
6 cups flour

Combine moist ingredients. Add dry ingredients gradually. Roll out, but not too thin. Cut out with cookie cutters and bake at 350 degrees for 10 minutes.

60

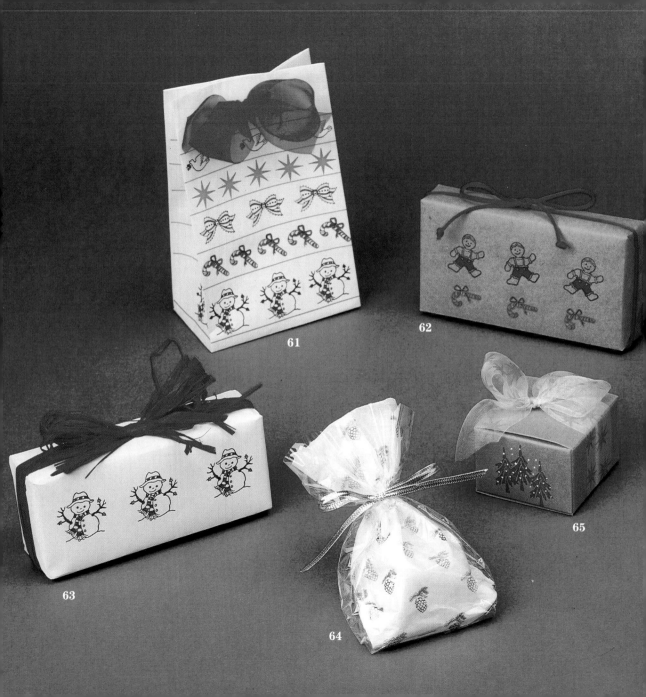

61

62

63

64

65

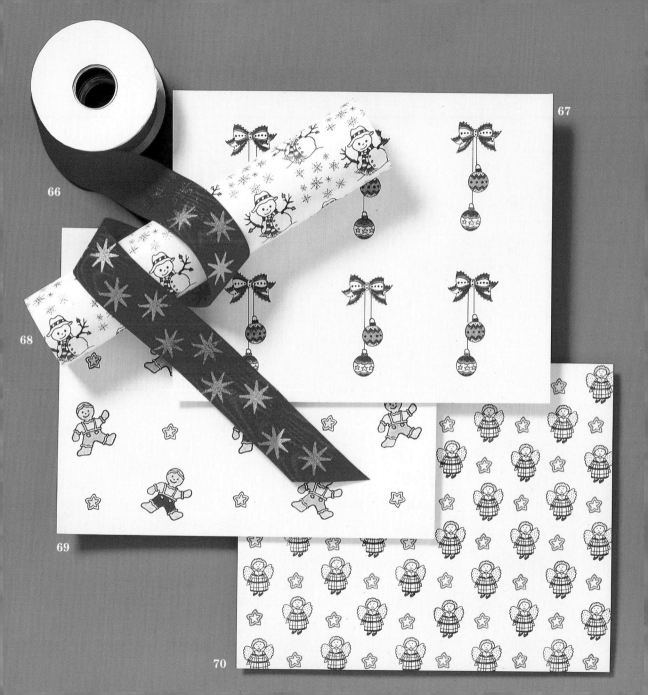

66

67

68

69

70

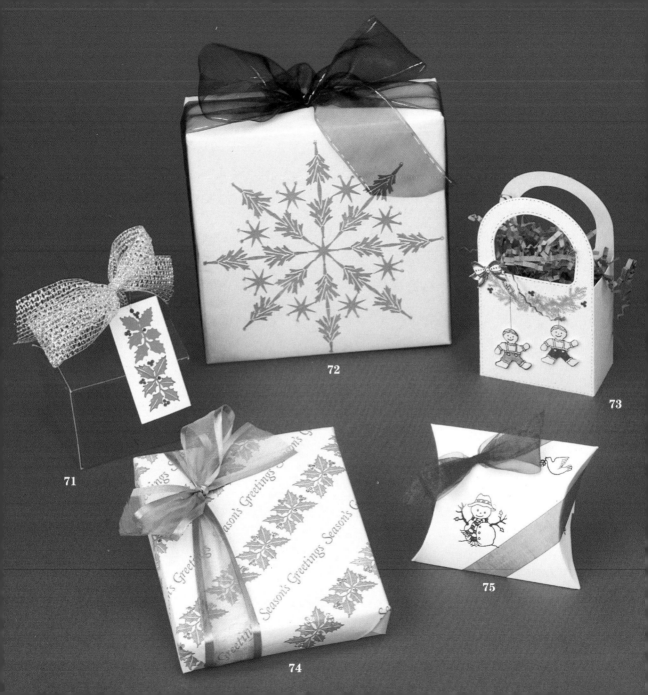

71

72

73

74

75

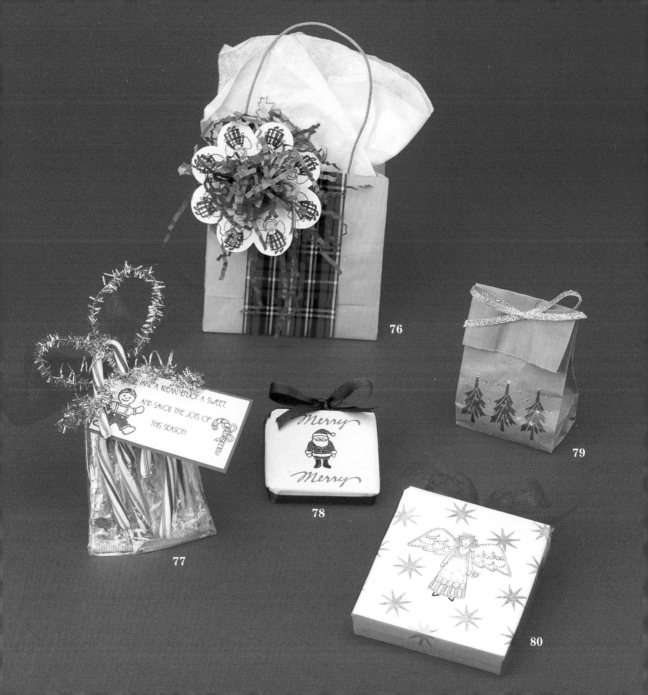

76

77

HAVE A HEART, ENJOY A SWEET,
AND SAVOR THE JOYS OF
THIS SEASON!

78

Merry

Merry

79

80

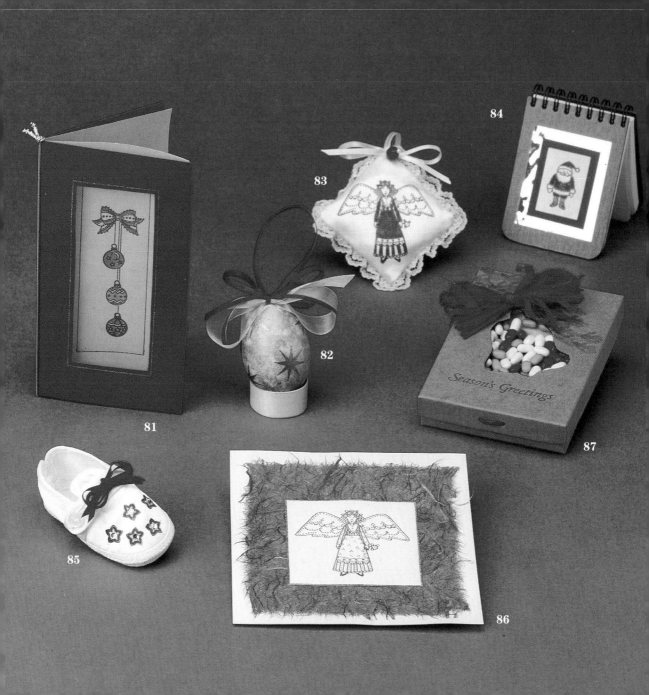

81

83

84

82

85

Season's Greetings

87

86

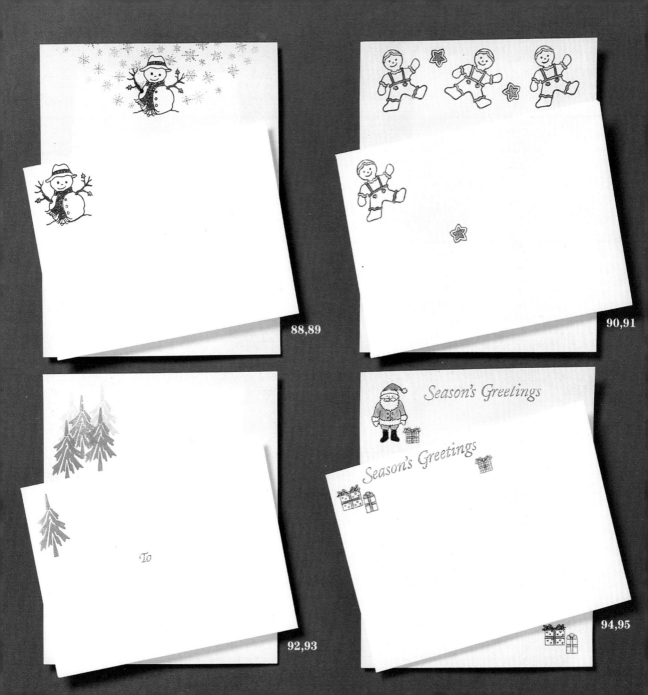

88,89

90,91

92,93

To

Season's Greetings

Season's Greetings

94,95

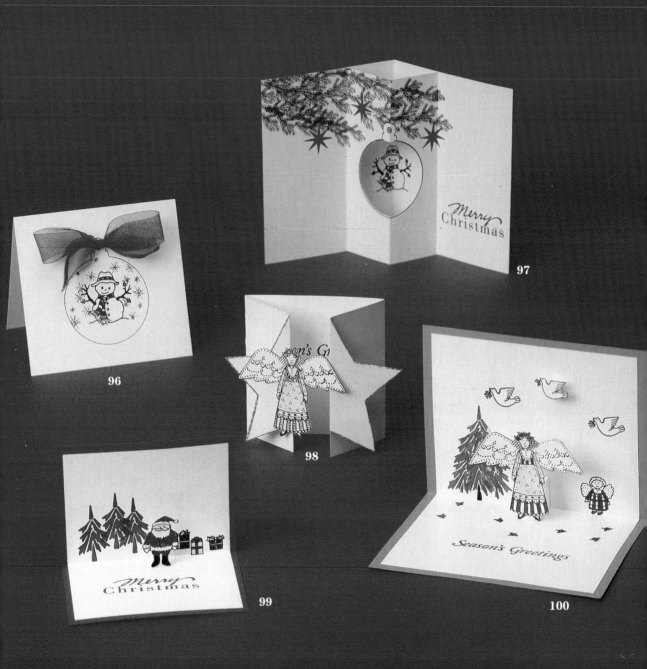

96

97

98

99

100

Project Number 1

STAMPS: *Tree, Dove*

SUPPLIES: *Black & Green Markers, Gold Glitter Glue, Card, Masking Paper & Scissors*

TIPS & TECHNIQUES: Use markers to apply green ink to the tree and black ink to the stem of the tree. Stamp in the center of the card, near the bottom. Ink the dove with black and stamp it in the center near the top of the card. Mask the dove. Ink only the green portion of the tree stamp (not the stem) and stamp it directly under the dove, with the tip of the tree printing on the mask. Using the sample as your guide, stamp the two bottom outside edges of the tree. Fill in the balance of the tree by repeatedly inking and stamping the tree. You will obtain a more natural look if you do not always ink the entire tree stamp and if you vary the portion of the stamp you ink. Ink the holly on the dove stamp with a black marker to decorate the tree. Apply gold glitter glue on top of the holly and create the glitter border.

Project Number 2

STAMPS: *Small Angel, Small Star*
SUPPLIES: *Black, Red, & Green Markers, Black Fine Point Marker, Gold Glitter Glue, Card, Masking Paper & Scissors*

TIPS & TECHNIQUES: This card was created by using a black marker to ink all the stamps. Stamp the angels, evenly spaced, onto your card, and cut a mask for the angel. Stamp the star stamp around the angels. To give dimension on your card stamp at least one star slightly over the masked angel to make it look as though it is behind the angel. Draw lines extending to the top of the card making the angels and stars into hanging ornaments. Color with the red and green markers. Add dots of gold glitter glue for sparkle.

Project Number 3

STAMPS: *"Season's Greetings," Small Star, Bow, Pine Bough, Pine Cone*

SUPPLIES: *Green Ink Pad, Black, Red, & Green Markers, Red Fine Point Marker, Gold Glitter Glue, Card, Masking Paper & Scissors*

TIPS & TECHNIQUES: Using a pencil draw a scalloped edge on the bottom of your card. It is easiest if you use something round, like a

coin, as a template. Cut around the scallops making the front of the card shorter than the back. Open the card and color in the lower portion of the card with your red marker so that when the card is closed the red shows behind the scallops. Using the black marker, stamp three bows across the card, and mask the bows. Create a garland across the card using the pine bough and the green ink pad. Add a pine cone on the garland under each bow using the black marker. Color in the bows with your red marker. Stamp "Season's Greetings" inked with green and add a star inked in black. Color the star with your red marker. Using the red fine point marker, add dots to the edge of your scallops. Fill in the center of your star with gold glitter glue.

PROJECT NUMBER 4

STAMPS: *Pine Bough, Dove, Bow*

SUPPLIES: *Green Ink Pad, Black & Red Markers, Gold Glitter Glue, Card, Masking Paper & Scissors*

TIPS & TECHNIQUES: The wreath was created by first lightly drawing a circle with pencil on the center of the card. Try drawing around a glass or cup if you don't have a circle template. Stamp the bow and mask.

Using the pine bough start building your wreath following the circle you drew on the card. For variety, ink different portions of the bough each time you stamp. Build your wreath to the fullness you desire. Remember no two wreaths look the same. Ink the dove in black and stamp in the middle of the wreath. Draw a line suspending the dove inside the wreath. Color the bow red and decorate the wreath with gold glitter glue.

PROJECT NUMBER 5

STAMPS: *Large Angel, Small Star*

SUPPLIES: *Black Marker, Red & Green Colored Pencils, Gold Glitter Glue, Card, X-Acto Knife*

TIPS & TECHNIQUES: Ink the large angel in black and stamp in the center of your card. Stamp a star in each corner. Using a black fine tip marker, create a border by drawing lines to connect the stars. Color the angel and stars with your colored pencils. To lift the angel's wings, cut around the outside edge of each wing using an X-Acto knife. Do not cut where the wings meet the body. Gently lift her wings. Add gold glitter glue.

Project Number 6

STAMPS: *Ornaments, Small Star, Bow, Pine Bough*

SUPPLIES: *Green Ink Pad, Black, Red, & Green Markers, Yellow Colored Pencil, Card, Masking Paper & Scissors*

TIPS & TECHNIQUES: Stamp bows in the top left and right corners using black ink. Mask the bows. Build the garland using the pine bough and green ink. Using the green marker, go back and add tiny dots around your garland, to add interest and dimension. With the red marker ink the ornaments and stars and stamp them below the garland. Use the red fine point marker to draw lines attaching the decorations to your garland. Color the decorations and bows with your red marker and yellow colored pencil.

Project Number 7

STAMPS: *Tree, Santa, Snowman, Presents*

SUPPLIES: *Green Ink Pad, Black & Red Markers, Black Fine Point Marker, Card Stock, Glue or Double Stick Tape, Masking Paper & Scissors*

TIPS & TECHNIQUES: Cut card stock approximately 2 inches smaller in height and width than your card. All the stamping will be done on the small piece and then mounted on the card.

Ink the snowman using the black marker and stamp. Mask the snowman. Stamp the forest of trees using the ink pad. Start with the trees you want to appear closest, and repeat the tree higher without reinking to create an illusion of depth. Ink Santa with the black marker, and one present with red. Stamp another tree next to Santa that extends off the paper. Use a black fine point marker to draw lines under Santa and the trees. This will make them appear to be standing on the ground and not floating in space. Color Santa and the snowman's scarf with your red marker. To frame the card, hold the stamped card in one hand and your green marker in the other, and run the marker along the edge. Attach your stamped scene to the card using glue or double stick tape.

Project Number 8

STAMPS: *Bow, Pine Bough, "Season's Greetings," Holly on "To/From"*

SUPPLIES: *Green Ink Pad, Black, Red, & Green Markers, Red Fine Point Marker, Glue or Double Stick Tape, Card Stock, Masking Paper & Scissors*

TIPS & TECHNIQUES: Cut card stock larger than your photograph and mark, with a pencil, where you want the photograph. Ink the bow with a black marker and stamp one in each corner at the top of the card. Mask the bows. Stamp the pine bough inked in green around the bows. Stamp "Season's Greetings" in green at the center, close to the bottom of the card. Ink the holly leaves in green and the berries in red and stamp on each side of the greeting. Mount the picture onto the card using glue or double stick tape. Draw the border around the picture with the red fine point marker.

PROJECT NUMBER 9

STAMPS: *Ornaments, "Merry Christmas," Pine Cone*

SUPPLIES: *Black, Red, & Green Markers, Yellow Colored Pencil, Card, Green Raffia or Ribbon Bow, Glue, Cardboard, Embossing Tool, Bone Folder or Knitting Needle*

TIPS & TECHNIQUES: To make the frame of the card stand out, cut a piece of cardboard 2 inches by 3 inches. Open your card and lay the front face down over the piece of cardboard making sure it's in the center. With a blunt object such as an embossing tool, bone folder, or a knitting needle, gently press the outside of the card down by running the

embossing tool along the edge of the cardboard. This technique is called paper embossing. It works best if you hold it up to the window so you see the edge of the cardboard. Stamp "Merry Christmas" in the center of the card, inking "Merry" with the red marker and "Christmas" with the green marker. Do not ink the holly. Stamp a border of ornaments, inking each ornament separately with the black marker. Ink the bough portion of the pine cone, adding a sprig of green to the top of each ornament. Color the ornaments with red and green markers and a yellow colored pencil. Attach the bow of raffia or ribbon at the top of the card with glue.

PROJECT NUMBER 10

STAMPS: Bow, *"Handstamped by"*

SUPPLIES: *Red & Green Markers, Card*

TIPS & TECHNIQUES: Stamp the bow, inked with a red marker, in the center of the card. Stamp "Handstamped by" below the bow in green. Decorate the bow with the green marker. Don't forget to add your name or initials to the card.

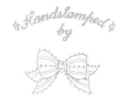

PROJECT NUMBER 11

STAMPS: *Bold Star, Dove, Holly on "To/From"*

SUPPLIES: *Black, Red, & Green Markers, Green Fine Point Marker, Gold Glitter Glue, Card Stock, Ruler*

TIPS & TECHNIQUES: The first step is to measure and create the nine-box grid with dots using a green fine point marker. Each box on the sample is 1 inch square with a 1/2-inch-wide frame. Next stamp the dove and bold stars, alternating boxes. Ink the bold star in green and the dove in black with the holly in green and berries in red. Using the holly portion of the "To/From" stamp, ink the leaves in green and the berries in red. First stamp the holly once in each corner and then fill in the border alternating the direction of the holly. You may wish to ink only the leaves of the holly, and then, after stamping, draw the berries with a red fine point marker. Draw a final border around the outside of the card with the green fine point marker and decorate with gold glitter glue.

PROJECT NUMBER 12

STAMPS: *Large Angel, Bold Star*

SUPPLIES: *Green Ink Pad, Black Marker, Red, Yellow, & Green Colored Pencils, Card, Masking Paper & Scissors*

TIPS & TECHNIQUES: Stamp the angel, inked in black, in the center of your card. Mask the angel, open the card, and also mask the back of the card to keep it free of images. Stamp the solid star repeating it to create a background design. Color the angel with the colored pencils.

PROJECT NUMBER 13

STAMPS: *Large Angel*

SUPPLIES: *Black Marker, Red Fine Point Marker, Red, Yellow, & Green Colored Pencils, Glue or Double Stick Tape, White & Colored Card Stock, Ruler, Pencil, X-Acto Knife*

TIPS & TECHNIQUES: Stamp the large angel in the center of the card. In pencil, lightly draw a square around the angel just inside her wings and feet. Draw another square 3/8 inch inside the first square. Cut on both of these lines with your X-Acto knife. Cut around the angel's wings and dress but do not cut across the portions of the feet or wings that extend beyond the lines. Mount the card on the red paper. Draw a frame around the angel with the red fine point marker and color with the colored pencils.

PROJECT NUMBER 14

STAMPS: *"Merry Christmas," Bold Holly*

SUPPLIES: *Green & Red Markers, Green Fine Point Marker, Glue or Double Stick Tape, Card Stock*

TIPS & TECHNIQUES: Cut the card larger than your photograph and mark, with a pencil, where you wish to place it on the card. Using a portion of the bold holly stamp ink the leaves with the green marker and the berries with red. Stamp at each corner of the photo. Now ink only one leaf at a time and stamp it randomly around the sides and top of the card. With the green fine point marker, connect the holly leaves with a wavy line of dashes. With your red marker, draw holly berries along the wavy line. With the red and green markers, ink the "Merry Christmas" but do not ink the holly. Stamp it on the bottom of the card. Attach the photograph with glue or double stick tape.

PROJECT NUMBER 15

STAMPS: *Dove, Holly on "To/From"*

SUPPLIES: *Black, Red, & Green Markers, Black & Red Fine Point Markers, Card Stock*

TIPS & TECHNIQUES: Lightly, pencil a heart shape on the card. Using your penciled line as a guide, stamp the dove, inked with black, and the berries in red, on the card. Color the holly leaves with the green marker. Stamp the holly portion of the "To/From" stamp in the center using the red and green markers to ink the stamp. Draw lines with the black fine point marker to hang the holly from the heart. Draw a border around the card with the red fine point marker. If you have difficulty spacing the doves evenly, read the section about using a stamp positioner.

PROJECT NUMBER 16

STAMPS: *Bold Holly*

SUPPLIES: *Green Ink Pad, Gold Glitter Glue, Card Stock*

TIPS & TECHNIQUES: Stamp the bold holly in green three times across the card. Remember, for even spacing start with the center image and then stamp the images on each side. Draw parallel lines, one on each side of the holly with the gold glitter glue. Also put glitter glue on each holly berry.

PROJECT NUMBER 17

STAMPS: *Candy Cane, Small Star, Pine Bough*

SUPPLIES: *Green Ink Pad, Black & Red Markers, Red Fine Point Marker, Yellow*

Colored Pencil, Gold Glitter Glue, Card, Masking Paper & Scissors

TIPS & TECHNIQUES: Begin by stamping, in red, the candy cane three times horizontally across the card. Mask the candy canes and stamp the pine bough twice using the green ink pad, once in each direction behind the candy cane. Color in the bow with your yellow colored pencil. Stamp the small star below each candy cane in black. Color the star with red and draw lines from the stars to the candy canes. Apply gold glitter glue to the center of each star.

PROJECT NUMBER 18

STAMPS: *Gingerbread Boy, Candy Cane, Small Star*

SUPPLIES: *Red & Green Markers, Red, Yellow, & Green Colored Pencils, Red Fine Point Marker, Double Stick Foam Tape, White & Colored Card Stock, Scissors*

TIPS & TECHNIQUES: Stamp the candy cane three times across the bottom of the card with the red marker. Next stamp the small star in red in the top corners directly above the candy canes.

Stamp three stars between each candy cane, creating a garland. Draw lines between each star and the candy canes to form the frame. Color in the stars and the bows with the colored pencils. Stamp the gingerbread boy in black on contrasting paper and color him in with the colored pencils. Cut him out and attach him to the card with double stick foam tape. Mount the card on a contrasting piece of card stock to frame.

PROJECT NUMBER 19

STAMPS: *Pine Bough, Gingerbread Boy, Candy Cane, Small Star, Bow, Tiny Star on Ornament*

SUPPLIES: *Black, Red, & Green Markers, Black & Green Fine Point Markers, Yellow Colored Pencil, Die-Cut Stocking Ornament Card, Scissors*

TIPS & TECHNIQUES: The stocking on this card was created by tracing around the die-cut stocking ornament with the black fine point marker. Draw the heel and toe with the marker using the sample as a guide. Stamp inside with the tiny star in the ornament stamp inked in black. Make a mask of the stocking. Stamp the gingerbread boy in black and the candy cane in red so they are popping out of the stocking. Make masks for both and stamp the pine bough repeatedly around them. Add the bow at the cuff of the stocking inked with black. Suspend the small star from the bow by drawing a line with the fine point marker. Add the stitching lines using a fine point marker. Color with the red and green markers and yellow colored pencil.

PROJECT NUMBER 20

STAMPS: *Snowman, Candy Cane*

SUPPLIES: *Black & Red Markers, Red, Yellow, & Green Colored Pencils, Red Fine Point Marker, Card*

TIPS & TECHNIQUES: The first step is to measure and draw the six-box grid with a red fine point marker. Next stamp the candy cane, inked with the red marker, three times, alternating squares. Stamp the snowman in the other three squares using the black marker. Color in the snowman's hat and scarf and the bow on the candy canes with the red and yellow pencils; color the leaves on the snowman with the green pencil.

PROJECT NUMBER 21

STAMPS: *Gingerbread Boy, Small Star*

SUPPLIES: *Black, Red, & Green Markers, Deckle Scissors, Red Ribbon, White and Colored Card Stock, 1/8-inch Hole Punch, Stamp Positioner*

TIPS & TECHNIQUES: Cut a circle out of the red paper. For the sample we used deckle scissors, but similar results can be obtained using pinking or regular scissors. Cut a circle out of the white paper slightly smaller than the red circle. Stamp the gingerbread boy on the white paper at 12:00, 6:00, 3:00, and 9:00. Fill the spaces between each of these gingerbread boys with another. Stamp a star in the very center. Color in the gingerbread boys and the star with markers. Using a stamping positioner will ensure an even distribution of gingerbread boys. Mount the layers of paper together with double stick tape or glue. Punch two holes about 1 inch apart on the fold of the card. Thread the ribbon through the holes and tie a bow.

PROJECT NUMBER 22

STAMPS: *Large Angel*

SUPPLIES: *Black & Red Markers, Black Fine Point Marker, Green & Yellow Colored Pencils, Die-Cut Star Ornament, Card, X-Acto Knife*

TIPS & TECHNIQUES: Draw around the die-cut star and, using a copier, reduce the image until the desired size is achieved. Using the copy as a template, place it in the corner and draw around the star with a black fine point marker. Continue draw-

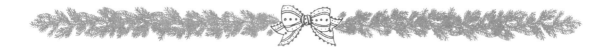

ing the frame of the card. Cut away the inside of the frame with your X-Acto knife. Stamp the angel in the center on the inside of the card so that she shows through the frame. Color her with the markers and pencils. Apply gold glitter glue around the inside of the star.

PROJECT NUMBER 23

STAMPS: *Bow, Holly on "To/From," Pine Bough*

SUPPLIES: *Black, Red, & Green Markers, Red Fine Point Marker, Card, Masking Paper & Scissors, X-Acto Knife*

TIPS & TECHNIQUES: This card was created using a tri-fold card. Stamp the bow diagonally just off center on the card. Mask the bow and stamp pine boughs around the bow. Draw dashes with a red fine point marker to form a rectangle diagonally in the center of the card. The rectangle should start and end at the bow and pine boughs. Using a ruler draw dashes from the rectangle across the card to the edge ending with the holly stamped in the corners. Continue the stitching lines to the top of the card. Add the solid holly inked with the red and green markers around the pine bough and across on the card. Using your X-Acto knife cut just below the stitching line fol-

lowing around the rectangle and pine bough across to the other side of the card. Add a message to the rectangle, open up, and write a letter on the inside.

PROJECT NUMBER 24

STAMPS: *Snowman, Candy Cane*

SUPPLIES: *Black, Red, & Green Markers, Red Fine Point Marker, White & Colored Card Stock, Glue or Double Stick Tape, Stamp Positioner*

TIPS & TECHNIQUES: Cut a piece of red paper about 1 inch narrower than the card, and then cut a piece of white paper about 1 inch narrower than the red paper. Stamp the snowman in black three times across the smallest white paper. Stamp the candy cane in red between the snowmen. Use the stamp positioner to line up these stamps exactly. Color in with the red and green markers. Draw a line across the paper about 1/4 inch from the edge with a red fine point marker. Mount the white paper to the red and then mount the red paper to the card with glue or double stick tape.

PROJECT NUMBER 25

STAMPS: *Gingerbread Boy, Small Star, "Merry Christmas"*

SUPPLIES: *Black, Red, & Green Markers, Brown Colored Pencil, Green Scroll & Brush Pen or Green Fine Point Marker, Card*

TIPS & TECHNIQUES: Stamp the gingerbread boy three times, in black, diagonally across the card. Rotate the gingerbread boy stamp slightly each time you stamp it to make him dance. Draw two green lines below the gingerbread boys diagonally across the paper. For this special pair of lines we used a scroll marker that has a thin line over a thicker line. If it is not available, draw two lines with a thin green marker. Cut the card just below the double line. Stamp the "Merry" portion of the "Merry Christmas" stamp in red, across the page. Remember to start in the middle and work toward the edge. Stamp the stars randomly around the gingerbread boys and color with the red and green markers. Color the gingerbread boy with the red and green markers and a brown colored pencil.

PROJECT NUMBER 26

STAMPS: *Santa, Snow*

SUPPLIES: *Black & Red Markers, White & Colored Card Stock, Glue or Double Stick Tape, Double Stick Foam Tape*

TIPS & TECHNIQUES: Cut a square out of the red paper about 2 inches smaller than the card. Cut the green paper about 1/2 inch smaller than the red, and the white 1/2 inch smaller than the green. Stamp the snow in black repeatedly all over the small white paper. Stamp Santa in black on white card stock and carefully cut him out. Color Santa with the red marker. Use glue or double stick tape to layer the paper and use foam tape to mount Santa so he hops out of the middle of the card.

PROJECT NUMBERS 27-38

TIPS & TECHNIQUES: These projects show many ways to create gift tags or tree ornaments using the die-cuts supplied with this kit. Let your imagination go wild. These were all created using techniques which we have already discussed. Remember to look at each component on a stamp separately. You may find images that you didn't even know existed.

PROJECT NUMBERS 39-47

TIPS & TECHNIQUES: Gift tags are a great way to get the whole family involved in the gift wrapping. These were all created using the supplies and techniques described in the book.

PROJECT NUMBERS 48-55

SUPPLIES: *Card Stock, Various Markers, X-Acto Knife, Bone Folder & Ruler*

TIPS & TECHNIQUES: These samples show just a few of the placecards that can be made. Many of these use a cutting technique where you measure the center line of the paper and lightly mark it. Stamp your images over the center line of the card. Score the card on the center line but do not score over the stamped images. Read about scoring in the pop-out section. Cut with your X-Acto knife from the score line up and over the design and back to the score line. When you fold the card, your stamped image will appear to pop up.

PROJECT NUMBER 56

STAMPS: *Bold Star*

SUPPLIES: *Wooden Bowl, White & Metallic Gold Acrylic Paint, Acrylic Spray Sealer or Spray Varnish, Foam Brush or Foam Piece*

TIPS & TECHNIQUES: Apply a white wash to the bowl using the white acrylic paint. (We rubbed the paint on with paper towels to get a very thin coating.) Apply gold acrylic paint to the bold star stamp with a small foam brush or put the paint on a piece of foam and use as a stamp pad. Stamp a random pattern on the wooden bowl. Clean your stamp between stampings if you find the image is becoming blurred. Apply gold paint to the rim of the bowl with the sponge brush. Seal the bowl with several coats of acrylic spray sealer or spray varnish.

PROJECT NUMBER 57

STAMPS: *Gingerbread Boy, Candy Cane, Small Star*

SUPPLIES: *Red & Black Markers, Yellow, Red, & Green Colored Pencils, Card*

TIPS & TECHNIQUES: Stamp the gingerbread boy three times across the card in black. Stamp the small star randomly in black across the top portion of the card and stamp the candy canes across the bottom of the card. Rotate the candy canes, stamping them in red at varied heights. Color with the yellow, red, and green colored pencils.

PROJECT NUMBER 58

STAMPS: *Bold Star*

SUPPLIES: *Cloth Napkin, Metallic Gold Acrylic Paint, Foam Brush, Cotton Swab*

TIPS & TECHNIQUES: Review the section on fabric stamping. It is helpful to first plan your layout on a piece of scrap paper the same size as the napkin. Ink the stamp with the foam brush and clean off any excess paint from the background with a cotton swab. You will want to clean your stamp often for the sharpest images. To make the images permanent, follow the directions provided with the paint.

PROJECT NUMBER 59

STAMPS: *Holly on "To/From"*

SUPPLIES: *Red and Green Markers, Red Fine Point Marker, Card Stock, Bone Folder & Ruler*

TIPS & TECHNIQUES: Stamp the holly from the "To/From" stamp in each corner of this place-card using the red and green markers. Draw dashes with the red fine point marker connecting the holly. This forms a border around the card.

PROJECT NUMBER 60

STAMPS: *Gingerbread Boy, Small Star*

SUPPLIES: *Black, Red, & Green Markers, Card Stock*

TIPS & TECHNIQUES: Decorate your recipe cards using stamps. These images were stamped with the black marker, and then colored in with the red and green markers.

PROJECT NUMBER 61

STAMPS: *Dove, Bold Star, Bow, Candy Cane, Snowman*

SUPPLIES: *Green Ink Pad, Black, Red & Green Markers, White Bag, Ribbon, Hole Punch*

TIPS & TECHNIQUES: Place a piece of cardboard inside the bag so you have a firm stamping surface. Draw a line with the red marker around the bottom of the bag. Stamp the snowman inked with the black marker above the line. Draw a line around the bag above the snowman and stamp the candy canes around the bag. Continue with this process until you get to the top of the bag. Color the designs with the markers. Fold the top over, punch two holes at the top in the center, thread the ribbon through the holes and tie a bow to close the package.

PROJECT NUMBER 62

STAMPS: *Gingerbread Boy, Candy Cane*

SUPPLIES: *Black, Red, Green Markers, Kraft Paper, Ribbon, Raffia, or Cording*

TIPS & TECHNIQUES: Cut the wrapping paper to the size desired to wrap the package. Decide where to place your stamps by wrapping the paper around the package and creasing the paper on the edges. When you take the paper off the box you will still see the creases which will guide you when you place your images. Stamp the gingerbread boy, in black, three times. Stamp the candy cane stamp in red under the gingerbread boys. Color with the red and green markers. Wrap your present and tie with red ribbon, raffia, or cording.

PROJECT NUMBER 63

STAMPS: *Snowman*

SUPPLIES: *Black, Red, & Green Markers, White Wrapping Paper*

TIPS & TECHNIQUES: Find the front of the paper using the same techniques as Project Number 62, then stamp the snowman three times across the package. Color with markers.

PROJECT NUMBER 64

STAMPS: *Pine Cone*

SUPPLIES: *Green & Black Markers, White Tissue Paper, Cellophane Bag, Gold Ribbon*

TIPS & TECHNIQUES: Lay the tissue paper down on top of another piece of paper to catch the excess. Stamp the pine cone after inking with the green and black markers. Stamp randomly over the entire piece of tissue paper. You will be able to see your images on both sides of the paper. Wrap your gift leaving one end free and place into the cellophane bag. Tie up with the gold ribbon.

PROJECT NUMBER 65

STAMPS: *Tree, Bold Star*

SUPPLIES: *Green Ink Pad, White Correction Pen, Small Cardboard Box, White Organdy Ribbon*

TIPS & TECHNIQUES: Flatten the box and stamp the tree three times on either end using the ink pad. If you are stamping a regular cardboard box that doesn't flatten, be sure to put something inside to give you a firm surface to stamp on. Once completely dry, decorate with the white out for the snow. Next stamp the bold star stamp randomly on the ribbon, again using the ink pad.

PROJECT NUMBER 66

STAMP: *Bold Star*

SUPPLIES: *Pigment Ink, Satin Ribbon*

TIPS & TECHNIQUES: Lay out a section of ribbon. Stamp the star stamp randomly along the ribbon. Emboss with gold embossing powder (see section on embossing). Continue in this manner until all the ribbon is decorated.

PROJECT NUMBERS 67-70

TIPS & TECHNIQUES: These various wrapping papers are made by using markers on the stamps and laying out the designs on a grid (see the section on repeated images). The final step is coloring the designs.

PROJECT NUMBER 71

STAMP: *Bold Holly*

SUPPLIES: *White Card Stock, Green & Red Markers*

TIPS & TECHNIQUES: Using the green and red markers, ink the bold holly stamp. Stamp twice onto the tag.

PROJECT NUMBER 72

STAMPS: *Tree, Bold Star*

SUPPLIES: *White Wrapping Paper, Gold Glitter Glue, Green Ink Pad*

TIPS & TECHNIQUES: To make this wonderful symmetrical snowflake, stamp the tree, inked with the green ink pad, at 6:00, 12:00, 3:00, then 9:00. Make sure that the tops of the trees touch. A stamp positioner is helpful if you have difficulty with this step. Then fill in between these trees with other trees. Next, turn the stamp around so that you stamp all the trees stem to stem. Finally fill in with the bold star. Apply gold glitter glue to all the outside points of the snowflake.

PROJECT NUMBER 73

STAMPS: *Pine Bough, Bold Holly, Gingerbread Boy, Bow*

SUPPLIES: *Green Ink Pad, Black, Red, & Green Markers, Die-Cut Gift Box, Glossy White & Tan Card Stock, Double Stick Foam Tape, Scissors*

TIPS & TECHNIQUES: Begin by stamping the garland using the pine bough stamp and ink pad. Adding tiny dots around your garland using the green marker will add interest and dimension to the design. Next, stamp the gingerbread boy twice, at different levels. On the tan card stock, stamp two gingerbread boys with the black marker. Stamp the bow inked with the black marker on the piece of white card stock. Cut out the boys and the bow after coloring them in with the green and red markers. Mount the two cut-out gingerbread boys with double stick foam tape being careful to position them exactly on top of the stamped images on the box. Mount the bow in the same way at the end of the garland.

PROJECT NUMBER 74

STAMPS: *Bold Holly, "Season's Greetings"*

SUPPLIES: *White Wrapping Paper, Green & Red Markers*

TIPS & TECHNIQUES: Ink the "Season's Greetings" stamp with the red marker and, using the grid, stamp in continuous slanted rows (see the section on repeated images). Using this row as a guide, ink the holly with the red and green markers and stamp above and below this line. Continue in this manner until the paper is covered.

PROJECT NUMBER 75

STAMPS: *Snowman, Dove*

SUPPLIES: *Black, Red, & Green Markers,*

Collapsible Glossy Gift Box

TIPS & TECHNIQUES: Stamp the snowman and the dove with the black marker. Color in the scarf red, and the dove's branch green. Voila!

PROJECT NUMBER 76

STAMPS: *Small Angel*

SUPPLIES: *Black Marker, Red & Green Fine Point Markers, Kraft Bag, White Card Stock*

TIPS & TECHNIQUES: For this "flower" to be symmetrical, it is important to lay out the angels evenly. Begin by stamping at the 6:00, 12:00, 3:00, and 9:00 positions on the card. The angel is inked with the black marker. Fill in between each angel with another angel. Color the angels using the fine tipped markers, alternating the red and green to make your plaid dress to coordinate with the plaid ribbon used on the bag. Finally, using a coin or other round object as a template, draw and cut a scalloped edge around the angels.

PROJECT NUMBER 77

STAMPS: *Gingerbread Boy, Candy Cane*

SUPPLIES: *White & Red Card Stock, Red Marker, Yellow Colored Pencil, Double Stick Tape or Glue*

TIPS & TECHNIQUES: Stamp the gingerbread boy in black ink on the left of the card, and the candy cane with the red marker on the right. Color in the gingerbread boy and write your message in between. Cut the red card a bit larger than the white and glue together so that there is a red border around your card.

PROJECT NUMBER 78

STAMPS: *Santa, "Merry Christmas"*

SUPPLIES: *Black & Red Markers, White Wrapping Paper*

TIPS & TECHNIQUES: Using the black marker, ink Santa and stamp him in the center of your paper. Color in his red suit. Ink the "Merry" of "Merry Christmas" with the red marker and stamp above and below Santa. Wrap your gift!

PROJECT NUMBER 79

STAMPS: *Tree*

SUPPLIES: *Green Ink Pad, Brown Paper Bag, Gold Glitter Glue, Gold Ribbon*

TIPS & TECHNIQUES: Stamp the green tree across the bottom of the small bag. Apply glitter to the tree tops and sparingly to the trees themselves. Fold the top of the bag over once, punch two holes, and tie a gold ribbon through the holes.

PROJECT NUMBER 80

STAMPS: *Large Angel, Bold Star*

SUPPLIES: *White Wrapping Paper, Green Ink Pad, Black Marker, Red & Yellow Colored Pencils*

TIPS & TECHNIQUES: Stamp the angel in the middle of your wrapping paper with the black marker. Stamp the stars randomly around her. Color in the angel using the colored pencils.

PROJECT 81

STAMPS: *Bow, Ornaments*

SUPPLIES: *Pigment Ink Pad, Gold Embossing Powder, Heat Gun, Red & Green Markers, Embossing Pen, Colored Card Stock, Vellum Paper, Gold Elastic Cord, X-Acto Knife*

TIPS & TECHNIQUES: Mark and cut a window out of the center of your colored card stock. Mark the outline of this window on the vellum. Ink each ornament separately with pigment ink, stamp on the vellum and emboss. Stamp the bow and emboss. With the embossing pen, draw lines connecting the ornaments to the bow and draw a frame slightly smaller than the inside of the window. Emboss this line. Draw lines 1/16 inch around the window on the colored stock and emboss the lines. Color on the reverse side of the vellum for a

stained glass effect. Attach the vellum to the card stock with gold elastic cord.

PROJECT NUMBER 82

STAMPS: *Bold Star*

SUPPLIES: *Pigment Ink, Gold Embossing Powder, Burgundy Ink, Sponge, Heat Gun, Tissue Paper, White Glue, Ribbons, Hot-Glue Gun*

TIPS & TECHNIQUES: Read the section about stamping on wood and other surfaces for the detailed instructions. We used burgundy ink to sponge the background of the egg, and gold embossing powder on the stamped tissue paper. Use ribbon to hang the ornament on the tree.

PROJECT NUMBER 83

STAMPS: *Large Angel*

SUPPLIES: *Black Pigment Ink, Clear Embossing Powder, Red & Yellow Fine Point Fabric Markers, Shiny Off-White Fabric, Lace, Ribbons, and Trims, Small Embroidery Hoop, Needle and Thread, Heat Gun*

TIPS & TECHNIQUES: Take a piece of fabric larger than the piece needed for the ornament. For the best results, place the fabric in an embroidery hoop to hold it firm. Turn the hoop over so that the fabric is closest to the stamping surface. This should be the right side of your fabric. Stamp the large angel using black pigment ink and emboss with clear embossing powder. Color the angel with fabric markers. Cut the fabric to the desired shape, sew and stuff with cotton. Attach a ribbon to hang the ornament on the tree.

PROJECT NUMBER 84

STAMPS: *Santa*

SUPPLIES: *Small Notebook Covered with Brown Kraft paper, Black Pigment Ink, Clear Embossing Powder, Red Marker, Flesh Colored Pencil, Red & Off-White Card Stock, Gold Sticker Paper, Heat Gun, Glue or Double Stick Tape, Scissors or Paper Cutter*

TIPS & TECHNIQUES: Using the Santa stamp, ink the Santa with black pigment ink, stamp it on off-white card stock amd emboss with clear embossing powder. Color Santa, and cut out to the size you want. Glue it on a piece of colored card stock and then glue onto the gold sticker paper. Peel off the backing and stick it on the book. A perfect place to keep your Christmas list!

PROJECT NUMBER 85

STAMPS: *Small Star*

SUPPLIES: *Black Pigment Ink, Clear Embossing Powder, Red Fine Point Fabric Marker, Sew-on Rhinestones , Ribbon, Satin Baby Shoes*

TIPS & TECHNIQUES: Flatten out the shoe so you are stamping on a flat surface. If the garment you are stamping cannot be flattened out, stuff it firmly or place a hard object inside to support the stamping surface. Ink the star with black pigment ink and emboss with clear embossing powder. Emboss one star at a time. Color the outline area of the star with a red fabric marker. Securely sew on a rhinestone in the center of each star. Attach a ribbon to the shoe and your little one is ready for the holidays.

PROJECT NUMBER 86

STAMPS: *Large Angel*

SUPPLIES: *Pigment Ink, Gold Embossing Powder, Gluestick, Piece of Decorative Paper, Off-White Card Stock, Card, Heat Gun*

TIPS & TECHNIQUES: Use pigment ink to stamp the angel on a piece of card stock. Emboss the image in gold. Glue along the outside edges of the same card stock with a glue stick. Emboss the glue with gold embossing powder. It is best to work on one side at a time. Glue the piece of card stock to the decorative paper and attach both to your card.

PROJECT NUMBER 87

STAMPS: *"Seasons Greetings," Pine Bough*

SUPPLIES: *Green Ink Pad, Kraft Jewelry Box, X-Acto Knife, Clear Acetate, Bell-Shaped Ornament, Ribbon or Bow, Christmas Candy*

TIPS & TECHNIQUES: Use the bell-shaped die-cut ornament in your kit as a guide to draw the bell on the box top. Cut out the shape. Glue clear acetate to the inside of the box. Support the lid of the box with a firm object such as a book and stamp the pine bough stamp in green overlapping the stamp to construct a branch. Stamp "Season's Greetings" in green below the bell. Glue the bow on the box and it's ready to fill with bright Christmas candy.

PROJECT NUMBER 88, 89

STAMPS: *Snowman, Snow*

SUPPLIES: *Black, Red, & Green Markers, Stationery & Envelope, Masking Paper & Scissors*

TIPS & TECHNIQUES: Using the black marker, stamp the snowman at the center top of your stationery. Mask the snowman and stamp the snowflakes, also inked with the black marker, across the top of the paper. Remove the mask and the smiling snowman is in a blizzard. Stamp the snowman on the upper left corner of the envelope for a coordinated look. Color the snowman's hat and scarf with the red marker and the holly with the green marker.

PROJECT NUMBER 90, 91

STAMPS: *Gingerbread Boy, Small Star*

SUPPLIES: *Black & Red Markers, Red & Green Colored Pencils, Stationery & Envelope*

TIPS & TECHNIQUES: Stamp the gingerbread boy in black three times at various angles so he appears to dance across your paper. He also gives a friendly wave on the outside of your envelope. Place the star stamp, inked in black, between the dancing boys and use it to brighten the address of the envelope. Color with the red marker.

PROJECT NUMBER 92, 93

STAMPS: *Tree*

SUPPLIES: *Green Ink Pad, Green Marker, Stationery & Envelope*

TIPS & TECHNIQUES: Stamp a forest on your stationery using green ink. Start with the trees that you want to appear closest, and repeat stamping the trees higher on the paper without re-inking. This creates an illusion of depth. Add a single tree to your envelope. Ink only the "To" on the "To/From" stamp with the green marker and stamp it near the first line of the address.

PROJECT NUMBER 94, 95

STAMPS: *Santa, Gifts, "Season's Greetings"*

SUPPLIES: *Black, Red, & Green Markers, Red, Yellow, & Green Colored Pencils, Stationery & Envelope*

TIPS & TECHNIQUES: Using your markers, ink Santa in black and stamp in the upper left corner of the stationery. Ink a gift in red and stamp next to Santa. Stamp "Season's Greetings" in green at the center top. Using markers, ink one gift in red and one in green and stamp in the lower right corner. Coordinate the envelope with a green "Season's Greetings" surrounded by the presents stamp stamped in red and green. Color in as you wish.

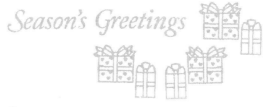

Project Number 96

STAMPS: *Snowman, Snow*

SUPPLIES: *Black, Red, & Green Markers, Ornament Gift Tag, Gold Glitter Glue, Glue, Black Fine Point Marker, Ribbon, Card, Masking Paper, Scissors*

TIPS & TECHNIQUES: Using the ornament gift tag or the frame from the gift tags, draw the ornament shape on the front of the card. Stamp the snowman in black in the center. Prepare a mortise mask for the outside of the ornament and a mask for the snowman. Stamp the snow around the snowman randomly. Some of the snow will fall over both masks. Remove the masks. Color as you wish and make the snow sparkle with the glitter glue. Tie the ribbon into a bow and attach with glue.

Project Number 97

STAMPS: *Snowman, Pine Bough, Bold Star, "Merry Christmas"*

SUPPLIES: *Green Pad, Green, Red, & Black Markers, Yellow Colored Pencil, Christmas Ball Gift Tag, Black Fine Point Marker, 2 Cards, Glue, X-Acto Knife, Masking Paper, Scissors, Bone Folder & Ruler*

TIPS & TECHNIQUES: Review the pop-out section for measuring and cutting the card.

Stamp the snowman on the second card so it can be seen easily through the hole cut in the first card. Stamp the bold star stamp in red and mask. Ink the pine bough stamp with the green pad and repeatedly stamp it to give the appearance of limbs of a large tree with the ball and the stars as ornaments. Ink the "Merry Christmas" stamp in green and red (do not ink the holly) and stamp it on the card. Color the snowman as you wish.

Project Number 98

STAMPS: *"Season's Greetings," Large Angel*

SUPPLIES: *Black & Blue Markers, Die-Cut Star Ornament (enlarged), Red & Green Colored Pencils, Gold Glitter Glue, Sponge, White Card Stock, Double Stick Tape or Glue, Scissors*

TIPS & TECHNIQUES: Stamp the angel in black on a piece of card stock and cut it out. Take another piece of card stock 10 1/2 x 3 1/2 inches, score and fold 1 3/4 inches in from each short end and again 1 3/4 inches from the previous fold. This leaves a 3 1/2-inch center. Fold the two end flaps back. Draw a star shape on the two end flaps. Cut the outside edges, leaving the star attached at the fold. One half of the star will be on each side. For the star shape we enlarged the star die cut ornament in the kit using a copier. Sponge

the background blue and mount the angel on either side of the front. Stamp "Season's Greetings" on the inside. Apply glitter glue to the edge of the star.

PROJECT NUMBER 99

STAMPS: *Santa, Tree, Presents, "Merry Christmas"*

SUPPLIES: *Black, Red, Green, & Blue Markers, Green Ink Pad, Yellow Colored Pencil, Glue or Double Stick Tape, Sponge, White & Colored Card Stock, Masking Paper, Scissors*

TIPS & TECHNIQUES: Review the section on pop-ups for preparation of the pop-up base. Ink Santa in black, stamp on card stock, color, and cut him out. Stamp trees in green. Sponge the sky in blue over a mask you have made in the shape of a cloud. Using the black marker, ink the gifts from the present stamp and stamp in the background. Ink the "Merry Christmas" stamp with red and green markers (do not ink the holly) and stamp it on the card. Color as you wish and attach the pop-up base, with Santa attached, to the card. Close the card you have stamped. Matching the fold-lines, apply glue to the outside edges of the white card and insert this card into the colored card stock.

PROJECT NUMBER 100

STAMPS: *Tree, Large Angel, Small Angel, Dove, "Season's Greetings"*

SUPPLIES: *Green Ink Pad, Black, Red, Green, & Blue Markers, Red, Green, & Yellow Colored Pencils, Glue or Double Stick Tape, White & Colored Card Stock, Sponge, Masking Paper, Scissors*

TIPS & TECHNIQUES: Review the pop-up and pop-out sections to construct the bases for the dove and the large angel. Stamp the dove and angel in black on the card stock, color and cut them out. Stamp a large tree using the tree and a green marker as outlined in Project Number 1. Ink, in black, the flower from the large angel and repeatedly stamp it on the bottom section of the card. Stamp two doves in the sky, mask them, and sponge light blue for the sky. Using black, stamp the small angel in the background. Assemble the pop-up angel and pop-out dove after coloring the images. Close the card and glue it inside the colored card stock matching the folds.

INDEX

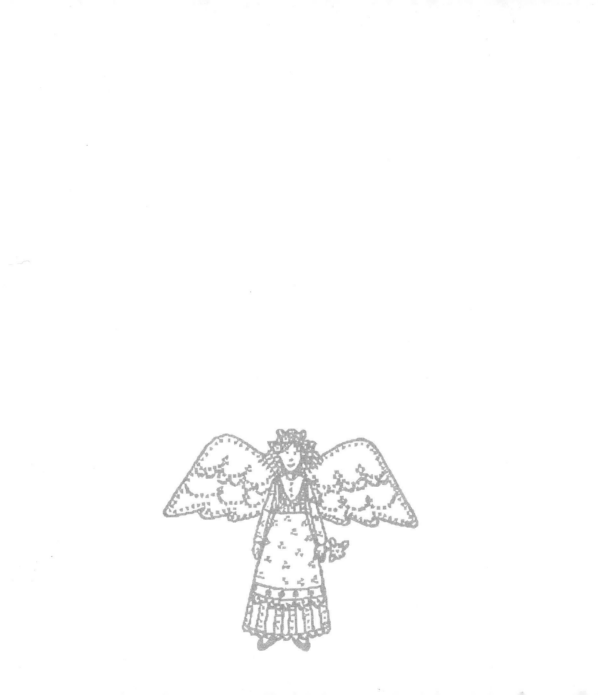